MANAGING CONFLICT

SAGE HUMAN SERVICES GUIDES, VOLUME 52

SAGE HUMAN SERVICES GUIDES

A series of books edited by ARMAND LAUFFER and CHARLES D. GARVIN. Published in cooperation with the University of Michigan School of Social Work and other organizations.

A **SAGE** HUMAN SERVICES GUIDE **52**

MANAGING CONFLICT

Herb BISNO

Published in cooperation with the University of Michigan School of Social Work

SAGE PUBLICATIONS
The International Professional Publishers
Newbury Park   London   New Delhi

DEDICATION

To my wife, Ziona

For information address:

SAGE Publications, Inc.
2455 Teller Road
Newbury Park, California 91320

SAGE Publications Ltd.
6 Bonhill Street
London EC2A 4PU
United Kingdom

SAGE Publications India Pvt. Ltd.
M-32 Market
Greater Kailash I
New Delhi 110 048 India

Printed in the United States of America

Library of Congress Cataloging-in-Publication Data

Bisno, Herb.
    Managing conflict.

    (Sage human service guides ; v. 52)
    Bibliography: p.
    1. Conflict management.   2. Human services.
I. Title.   II. Series.
HD42.B56   1988   361.3′2′068   88-1938
ISBN 0-8039-2585-9

SECOND PRINTING, 1991

CONTENTS

Part II: Managing Conflict

ACKNOWLEDGMENTS

I am indebted to La Trobe University, which, through its Outside Studies Program, provided me with an undisturbed period of time for research and writing. In addition, I was aided in bringing the manuscript to completion by the kindness of Dean Fred M. Cox, of the University of Wisconsin-Milwaukee, in providing me with support facilities. Also, Doris and Max Gendelman generously provided me with a "home away from home" during my sojourn in Milwaukee.

I am especially grateful to Carol Thurman, administrative officer, and Virginia Spriggs, Noelle Smart, and the other secretaries of the Social Work Department of La Trobe University for organizing and typing several drafts of the manuscript, while retaining their good humor and composure. In addition, Mary Ann Riggs and her associates at the University of Wisconsin-Milwaukee provided excellent secretarial assistance.

I wish to express particular appreciation to the coeditor of the Human Services Guide Series, Armand Lauffer, for sharing my belief in the importance of the subject matter of the book, and to the executive editor of Sage Publications, Charles T. Hendrix, for having expedited its publication.

I am greatly obligated to students and practitioners alike (both in Australia and the United States), for sharpening my ideas about the management of conflict and for their enthusiastic reception of the argument that this is a vital and legitimate aspect of professional practice. In addition, I have learned much from the personal experience of conflict in my professional life, although it must be said that some of those who contributed to my understanding of the subject did so quite unintentionally.

—Herb Bisno

INTRODUCTION

Human service organizations are not free of conflicts. Nor should they be. In fact, it is hard to conceive of any vital, responsive organization in a dynamic society being even relatively conflictless. Conflict is, after all, as natural as harmony, and it is difficult to envision the attainment of positive social goals (and even many personal ones) without it. Thus the intent of this volume is not to deplore conflict, per se, nor to call for its elimination. Rather, the focus is on the management of conflict so that its outcomes are as constructive as possible.

As we look around us, the effective and responsible regulation of conflict seems to be all too rare and the "costs," sometimes quite terrible, often blind us to the potential or actual benefits. In our workplaces, conflict is frequently defined in strictly negative terms, that is, as a source of aggression, frustration, despair, or resignation. Even human service organizations (including academic institutions) are not notable for their positive handling of conflictual situations. No wonder, then, that conflict has such a "bad name."

One objective of this book is to provide a corrective to the one-sided, negative, and "dysfunctional" image of conflict. To the contrary, conflicts of *interest* and *commitment* are an important, and sometimes positive, dimension of most aspects of human service work. For this reason, competence in coping with such conflicts is an essential part of the professional responsibility of all human service workers.

A second objective is to contribute to an enhanced understanding of the nature of conflicts of interest and commitment, and of conflict management.

The final and most important objective is to provide a selective overview of strategies, tactics, and techniques used in managing conflict.

These action options are described and assessed in respect to criteria for use, probable efficacy, professional values, and social implications.

Many human service workers think of the management of conflicts of interest/commitment as being mainly relevant to the macro arena of practice. It is true, of course, that such conflicts are a vital aspect of the functions of the community developer, the administrator, the advocate, and the social activist. But what about the direct service worker? Most direct service workers function within an organizational context. They interact with colleagues, with superordinates and subordinates, and with representatives of other professions, as well as with special "publics" (e.g., citizen groups, legislators). These workers may also find themselves in conflict-of-interest situations with nonvoluntary clients. And there are even episodes of this type of conflict with voluntary clients, episodes that call for conflict management competencies rather than clinical skills. In addition, direct service workers sometimes get involved in conflictual interactions with persons who serve as "significant others" in the lives of their clients (e.g., friends, relatives, landlords, other "helpers").

The reality is that conflicts of interest and commitment play a significant part in the occupational lives of virtually all human service workers. There are, naturally, some differences in the extent and types of conflict management activities associated with various work roles. For instance, workers engaged in macro tasks are more frequently involved than those in micro practice in conflict management transactions in which both parties represent a formal constituency.

In turn, direct service practitioners are somewhat more likely to engage in nonsymmetrical conflict than macro workers (e.g., the worker representing the organization while the client acts solely in his or her own interest). Also, conflict management transactions at the micro level have a greater tendency than those in macro situations to be characterized by an intermingling of personalistic elements with the interests/commitment component.

However, the differences in conflict management associated with the various human service roles are overshadowed by the commonalities, commonalities that will be stressed throughout the guide.

This "guide" is intended to be useful to a wide array of human service practitioners and practitioners-to-be in many different organizational contexts. We believe it will also prove helpful to members of diverse community associations, including volunteer organizations and self-help groups, as well as to those working in political organizations and business enterprises.

PART I

THE NATURE OF CONFLICT AND CONFLICT MANAGEMENT

Chapter 1

CONFLICT MANAGEMENT AND THE HUMAN SERVICE WORKER

Conflict—is a theme that has occupied the thinking of man more than any other, save only God and love. In the vast output of discourse on the subject, conflict has been treated in every conceivable way.

—Anatol Rapoport

CONFLICT MANAGEMENT AS AN OCCUPATIONAL NECESSITY

If human service workers are to fulfill the full range of their professional responsibilities and functions, the willingness to engage in conflict transactions is essential. Conflict situations are frequently sources of intense frustration and discomfort, and they often entail significant risks. Yet they are as much a part of the job as is the provision of service in harmonious circumstances.

Conflicts are an integral part of the functions of the human service worker because differences of interest and commitment are virtually built into the job specifications, so to speak. Think of the potential for conflict in the relationship between a worker and an involuntary client, such as an antagonistic child abuser; in the activities of the human service worker serving as the advocate for controversial legislation; in the work of the community developer facing resistance by entrenched economic interests; in the relationships among members of multiprofessional teams, each of whom is "turf"-conscious; or in the day-to-day interactions among workers, supervisors, and administrators, each of whom may have different concerns and perceptions.

CONFLICTS OF INTEREST
AND COMMITMENT

Conflict manifests itself in a variety of shapes, sizes, and even disguises. It appears throughout the entire gamut of human interactions. However, our attention in this volume will be directed toward the management of certain types of work-related conflicts, that is, conflicts related to *interests* and *commitment*. Thus conflicts that are primarily of an intrapsychic nature, or rooted in the affective aspects of social relationships, will be of only peripheral interest to us. This also applies to conflicts that are essentially the product of exceptional ineptness in interpersonal skills. Such a statement of exclusions does not imply, however, that emotional factors, or difficulties in personal functioning, are absent in conflicts of interest or commitment. On the contrary, feelings about interests and beliefs often run very high indeed.

We are not limiting ourselves to a "model" of a nonexistent human being, that is, a rational, cognitive, person abstracted from such emotions as anger, hurt, envy, or pride. However, while recognizing that the different kinds of conflict are not "pure," nor separated from each other by hard and fast boundaries, we have chosen to focus on conflicts that have interests or commitments at their cores. The reason for this emphasis is that such matters are of particular importance in work-linked interactions.

MEANINGS

No doubt we have all experienced a certain amount of frustration when provided with a "formal" definition in answer to our query as to the meaning of a complex phenomenon. Perhaps that is, in part, because too much is expected from such definitions. Although this book follows tradition by starting with formal statements, the subsequent discussion will elaborate upon them. One caveat is in order at this point: Our definition and discussion will refer to *social* conflict, that is, conflict between persons. Thus intrapersonal conflict, and such struggles as those between human beings and nature, are excluded.

DEFINITION OF SOCIAL CONFLICT

Social conflict refers to a process of social interaction involving a struggle over claims to resources, power and status, beliefs, and other preferences and desires. The aims of the parties in conflict may extend from simply attempting to gain acceptance of a preference, or securing a resource advantage, to the extremes of injuring or eliminating opponents.[1] Obviously, the potential sources of conflict are almost infinite, and the objectives, scope, intensity, methods, number of participants, and outcomes may also vary greatly.

In the scholarly literature on social conflict, one encounters many attempts to refine the concept and to differentiate it from related ideas. Not all of these efforts at elaboration and refinement are particularly relevant for our purposes. However, the relationship of *competition* to *conflict* is worth discussing. Two distinctions between them are well grounded and useful. First, conflict, unlike competition, requires the *perception of opposition* to a person, social unit (e.g., ethnic group, organization, class, or nation), or belief system. The second point of differentiation is that conflict may be engaged in over virtually anything, from basic interests to trivial preferences, or matters of largely emotional meaning. Competition, though, implies a process directed toward significant goals, such as the attainment of interests, or the dominance of beliefs to which one has a commitment, thus excluding many types of concern about which there may be conflict. This suggests, too, that although competition is not automatically conflict, it often results in conflict.

Two examples will help to clarify these distinctions. Let us suppose, in the first situation, that you are in competition with other people, many of whom were unknown to you, for a job (or a place in an academic program). Despite this competition you may not view your competitors as actual adversaries with whom you are locked in conflict.

In the second situation, imagine that you and your "life" partner (for the evening or an indefinite period) are having a heated, albeit trivial, dispute as to how you should dress for a dinner party. This is conflict, but not competition.

DEFINITION OF INTEREST

Since the focus in this volume is centered on conflicts of *interest* and *commitment,* we had better continue with our definitional excursion a bit longer so as to ensure a common ground of meaning in respect to these key terms. And, as is so often the case, the complexities of the concepts sneak up on us. At first glance they appear to be quite straightforward, but, upon reflection, the obvious becomes less so, the simple more complicated, and the assumed turns out to be problematic. This process is particularly applicable to the idea of "interest." In a psychological sense interest may be defined as persistent attention to, and preference for, some object or activity, due to the perceived attractiveness or desirability of that which is sought after. Although cast in less formal terms, this is essentially the same meaning attributed to the concept by Fisher and Ury (1981), who define interests as comprising desires and concerns. They maintain that interests "motivate people; they are the silent movers behind the hubbub of conflicting positions." So far so good—but is that really all there is to it? Are interests entirely a matter of subjective determination, or do they have a "reality" beyond one's perceptions? For instance, what is implied about the concept when a person tells you that it is in *your interest* to vote for candidate Z? Surely, this usage suggests that interest refers to an objective advantage that you may gain by taking a given action. This notion of an objective interest can be further extended by arguing that interests adhere to the positions and roles (i.e., economic status, gender, occupational role, etc.) people occupy. In other words, there are also structural determinants of interests. Thus people in varying social situations, and the incumbents of positions, may have different, and even conflicting, interests (e.g., buyer-seller, client-administrator of the agency).

Recognition of the objective aspects of interest is important and useful, but it also poses some difficult questions. One of these is whether, based on some objective criterion, persons may be said to misperceive their interests. For example, some observers would argue that this is what occurs when an impoverished individual consistently votes for a conservative political party that is basically unsympathetic to the plight of the poor. Such a claim assumes that an individual's (or a group's) real interest may be correctly identified by an outside observer, even though not recognized by the person whose interest is at issue.

DEFINITION OF FALSE CONSCIOUSNESS
AND PSEUDO-INTERESTS

The incorrect perception of one's (individual or collective) objective interests has been referred to as "false consciousness," particularly by writers in the Marxist tradition.[2] Another term that is sometimes employed to convey essentially the same idea, but is free of any particular ideological coloration, is *pseudo-interests* (Zollschan & Hirsch, 1964, p. 132). However, the central idea behind both of these concepts has been seriously challenged. Among the major criticisms are the following: (1) Interests don't exist except as perceived by the persons concerned; (2) specific interests don't automatically reside in social positions; (3) interests may be of very diverse character and the claim of false consciousness usually refers to just one category of "interest" (e.g., economic), overlooking the multiplicity of interests simultaneously held by individuals or groups; (4) the criteria for identifying "objective interests" are often unclear or arbitrary; and (5) it is elitist and arrogant to claim that the observer "knows" better than the person in question what that person's "real" interests are.

There is much merit in these criticisms. For example, a person's psychological interest (e.g., identification with a client group) may be expressed by behavior that, to an observer, does not appear to be in that individual's objective economic interests. In such an instance the issue is more a question of the person's *priority* of interests than it is of false consciousness. Or the values of the actor may simply be different from those of the observer. Yet, even granting the validity of various of the arguments challenging the concepts of false consciousness and pseudo-interests, these terms do highlight a reality that cannot be ignored. They convey an important truth that is vital for a realistic analysis of conflict and its management. For instance, "consciousness raising," which has been a useful device for feminists and other change-oriented groups, is implicitly based on the assumption that a type of false consciousness can, and does, exist. The efforts to change a "slave mentality" into an activist one also implies much of the same. Certainly, throughout history, individuals and groups have made choices that proved to be incompatible with their expressed goals. Furthermore, perceptions of interests have indeed been altered by new perspectives introduced from the outside.

Pause for Reflection

(1) We have all known of situations in which people appear to "change" after having been transferred or promoted to another position in the organization. Consider, for example, the following situation: Worker X, when a member of the adoptions unit, had fought hard for additional funds for that service. However, after transferring to the juvenile protection division, the same worker became an articulate advocate for more resources for *that* service, claiming it was unfairly treated when compared to other units, such as adoptions. Is this "change" an example of the relationship between position and interest?

(2) Do you think that the "acceptance" by many women, over the years, of the vow to *obey* their husbands, as part of the marriage ceremony, is an example of "false consciousness?"

Although the idea of false consciousness (or pseudo-interests) is useful, it should be employed with sensitivity and restraint because of the difficulties associated with the concept, and the fact that it is easily abused. There is a real danger in employing the label "false consciousness" as a weapon with which to attack ideological opponents, or to make a "point" in a dispute. Equally unwise is the use of the notion to "put down" others, or consciously to demonstrate superior insight and understanding. However, the concept can be of real assistance in understanding conflicts, or their absence, and in developing appropriate policies, strategies, and tactics.

An extension of the meanings we have attributed to the idea of interests is that of a claim, such as the right to participate in a relevant activity. For example, students may argue that they should be involved in curriculum decision making because they have a stake—that is, an interest—in the quality and substance of their education. Likewise, employees in an organization may argue that, since they have an interest in the selection of a new director, they should be allowed to influence the decision. So, too, clients may argue that they should participate in the policymaking activities of an agency, since they have a vital interest in the impact of such policies.[3]

SELF-INTEREST AND SELFISHNESS DIFFERENTIATED

Acting in one's own interest is not automatically undesirable, inappropriate, or unethical for a human service worker or organization. The discomfort that is frequently engendered in social workers and those in related occupations by the term *self-interest* is due not only to a misunderstanding of certain of their responsibilities and roles, but also to a tendency to equate *self-interest* with *selfishness*.

Self-interested actions may have prosocial outcomes, or they may be selfish in the sense of a narrow preoccupation with self to the exclusion of the well-being of others. For instance, if an individual gets gratification from helping other people, then providing such assistance is in the "self-interest" of the helper, since this behavior provides pleasure. But the assistance may also benefit the recipients if the help is appropriate. In such a situation, self-interest and the welfare of others are not in conflict. Of course, we can also think of persons who appear to define self-interest selfishly, that is, in a nonsocial or antisocial manner. However, since it is perfectly reasonable for human beings to seek realization of their interests, our concern ought to be with the substance of such self-interests and the effects of achieving these interests on others. There is nothing to be gained by denying the legitimacy of *self-interest,* or by dismissing it as a dirty word and unworthy motive.

DEFINITION OF COMMITMENT

The last part of our definitional exercise can be relatively brief. Our concern in this volume is largely with the *conflicts* of *interest* and *commitment* that are likely to confront the human service worker. Since the previous definitional discussion only covered the concepts of "conflict" and "interest," the term *commitment* remains to be clarified. By *commitment* we mean a strongly held specific position or abstract belief. The term also implies conviction about the correctness or rightness of the position or belief.

One type of belief to which people tend to be strongly committed is *values.* Values are "core conceptions of the desirable within every individual and society" (Rokeach et al., 1979, p. 2). They tend to have a strong emotional as well as cognitive element. Values are not specific or concrete rules of conduct; they possess a symbolic and abstract quality of rightness, of goodness and correctness. They function as generalized standards by which judgments are made as to courses of action, and by which the behaviors of oneself and others are evaluated.

Values are also used to support positions, as well as to depreciate the claims of opponents in conflict situations. An example would be the emphasis put on "choice" by one side and the "sanctity of the embryo" by the other in the heated dispute over abortion policy. Consider, as well, the divergent value-based views about who should or should not receive "welfare."

Conflicts over highly emotive, abstract value commitments tend to be particularly difficult to resolve. Hence it is often useful to shift the terms of such disputes to more specific and manageable levels. Of course, conflicts may arise not only because of the presence or absence of given values but because of the different priorities attached to them.

Of particular significance is the fact that there are important differences in the values espoused by members of the various human service professions. Since many human service activities involve multiple occupational groups, conflicts among their value orientations are a fact of life. Illustrative of this are the conflicting value commitments between the organized medical profession in the United States and many other human service workers in respect to comprehensive public health care.

INTERESTS AND COMMITMENTS

What we believe about given issues, and the positions we take on them, may be linked not only to our more general philosophical/ideological views, but also to our interests. This doesn't mean, though, that beliefs are always rooted in social/economic interests. For example, it is not unusual for leaders of revolutionary movements to have come from the class that they are trying to topple from power. Note the affluent backgrounds of some of the radical youth leaders of the 1960s and 1970s.

In many instances there is a connection between interests and beliefs. It is not pure chance that members of the business community often advocate lower taxes and a contraction of welfare programs. In turn, the less well off in society are likely to support policies that provide them with economic and social benefits.

Why do advocates of social policies seldom link their own interests to the beliefs they espouse, even though they frequently accuse opponents of holding to beliefs that are self-serving? The reason for this is that the legitimacy of beliefs (particularly when posed as "moral values") is thought to be enhanced when they are considered to be "disinterested." Thus, in conflicts over such matters, each side tries to gain a psychological edge by proclaiming the "purity" of its beliefs.

THE RELATIONSHIP BETWEEN "HELPING" AND "FIGHTING"

Most human service workers have received considerable training in the development of helping skills. But few have received training in fighting or conflict management skills. There are, of course, some basic competencies that apply to both modes of practice. These include communication skills, sensitivity to the reactions of other persons, disciplined "use of the self," the ability to secure an appropriate form of rapport, and basic social-psychological understandings. However, there are also decisive differences in "helping" and "fighting" transactions, differences that require particular sets of knowledge and skills.

To appreciate these differences, it is useful to distinguish between "helping" and "instrumental" professional actions. We use the concept of helping behavior to refer specifically to those interactions between the worker and the user-of-service in which the provision of assistance (of many types) is sought, or genuinely accepted, by the recipient. This usage excludes assistance that is objected to or perceived as an unwanted imposition. Instrumental behavior, defined as the other side of the coin, includes those "task-oriented" aspects of social work practice that are not, basically, of a helper-helped character.[4] The distinction between the two concepts is summarized in Chart 1.1.

The differentiation between the helping and instrumental functions is particularly important for the purposes at hand because the activities associated with the management of conflicts of interest and commitment most commonly fall within the instrumental category. Of course, there is no hard and fast dividing line between the helping and instrumental processes. They may, on occasion, overlap, blur, or even be used in the

CHART 1.1
Some Defining and Differentiating Characteristics of the
Helping and *Instrumental* Activities/Relationships

Helping	Instrumental

Goals in the Relationships

Goals usually shared between the worker and user-of-service.

Goals in the Relationship

Worker's goals may be different from, in conflict with, or similar to that of inter-actant.

Interests

Interests of worker and user-of-service are usually shared/similar.

Interests

Interests of worker and interactant may be in opposition or competition, or simply different, or be shared/similar.

Primacy of Responsibility

The primary responsibility and ethical obligation of the worker is to the user-of-service, although other accountabilities (such as to agency) are also involved.

Primacy of Responsibility

The primary responsibility of the worker will vary with the situation; it may be to the community, profession, colleagues, agency, social movement, reference group, user-of-service (or potential user-of-service), or to oneself (in a professional or employee role).

Authority, Control/Dependency

There tends to be a built-in imbalance in the helper-helped relationship in terms of authority (expertise) psychological control/dependency and the nature of the exchange process

Authority, Control/Dependency

There may be balance between them or greater dominance on the part of either the worker or the interactant. The worker is neither "automatically" in control of the situation nor necessarily invested with the greater authority.

Motivation

The user-or-service is usually motivated to enter into the relationship by a desire for assistance/provision of some resource (material or nonmaterial).

Motivation

The interactants may be motivated to enter into the relationship by virtually any "voluntary" motive, or by coercion. Among the motives may be the desire to gain an advantage (e.g., material gain, policy, professional, ideological, power, status, or to expedite a 'task'). In involuntary situations, legal or other coercive considerations may be responsible for the establishment of the relationship.

(continued)

CHART 1.1 Continued

Helping	*Instrumental*
Type of Relationship: Social/ Psychological Characteristics	**Type of Relationship: Social/ Psychological Characteristics**
The relationship between the worker and user-of-service is frequently of a "primary," or mixed primary/secondary character, although it may, in some instances, be almost entirely secondary. There often is considerable emphasis on "feeling states," as well as overt behavior.	The relationship between the worker and interactant is frequently (but not always) secondary and segmental. Emotional maintenance activities tend to be subordinated to task-related functions.
Relationship Model	**Relationship Model**
The relationship between the worker and user-of-service is usually perceived, explicitly or implicitly, as being essentially consensual.	The worker-interactant relationship is frequently seen as conflictual or competitive, although it may also be cooperative or supportive.
Nature of the Knowledge Guiding Interaction	**Nature of the Knowledge Guiding Interaction**
The worker tends to emphasize knowledge about the user-of-service that is particularistic—that is, gained from the user-of-service or from the records or other sources about the user-of-service. "Unique" (individual) aspects of the user-of-service are frequently focused upon and serve as the basis for the interpretation and prediction of behavior. The theoretical knowledge base is linked to all of the aforementioned characteristics of this type of relationship.	The worker frequently lacks much knowledge of the interactant as a person or unique entity; hence there may have to be considerable reliance on an understanding of general (shared) socialpsychological processes and overt behavioral responses as the basis for the interpretation and prediction of behavior. The theoretical knowledge base is linked to all of the aforementioned characteristics of this type of relationship.

same transactions or situations. Nevertheless, the distinctions between these two types of interaction are genuine and are important for an understanding of the relationship (and stresses) between the helping and fighting functions of the human service worker.

As an instrumental activity, conflict management has certain basic defining characteristics that differentiate it from the helping function. To begin with, in a conflict situation the goals and interests of the human service worker and the interacting adversary (who may even be another such worker) are often different, or even opposing. For example, a social worker in a mental health setting wants more power in the decision-making process as to the treatment a client will receive, while the team leader, a psychiatrist, resists this demand. Thus a conflict ensues. In this situation the occupational and personal goals of the adversaries are in opposition. The interests of the social worker reside in securing greater recognition, both for self and profession. However, the psychiatrist's predominate interest is in defending the greater authority and prestige afforded psychiatry and self as a member of that occupation.

Another example of clashing goals may be when the objective of a worker is to have his or her involuntary client cooperate in order to utilize the agency's services in a constructive matter. The worker's interest in the matter is to be effective as well as to appear to be so to others in the organization, and to minimize aggravation and the expenditure of time. However, the client's goal may be to have as little to do as possible with the agency, thus promoting his or her interests, which are self-perceived as being freedom from unwarranted and unwanted interference by the worker and the organization the worker represents.

In the above examples, the parties, in striving for respective goals, are seeking the attainment of their differing interests. Of course, even in conflict situation some of the interests of the parties may be shared. For instance, in the first example, that of the social worker and psychiatrist in conflict, both may genuinely share an interest in the provision of good service to clients. But their differing views of what decision-making pattern will result in this outcome reflect opposing interests and commitments.

In contrast, the interests and goals of the worker and client in a helping situation are more likely to be congruent. This is because the overall goal, the client's well-being, is usually shared by the worker. Of course, even in a cooperative type of interaction, differing definitions of the situation between worker and client may exist. For instance, in a marriage counseling situation, mutual adjustment by both partners may be the primary interest of the worker, whereas each marital partner may wish to put all the blame for the marital tensions on the other partner. In this situation, the worker may define the client's wishes as mistaken, misplaced, or preliminary, that is, subject to change with growth. Despite the lack of perfect symmetry in their perceptions, the goals and interests are shared by both worker and client to a much greater extent, and at a more essential level, than in the examples given of conflict-type situations.

Congruity in the goals of the parties is also built into the helping situation by the ethically mandated preeminence of the client's interests. In other words, our primary responsibility as human service workers is to the well-being of the client, although other interests (e.g., organizational, "public interest") do play some part. This contrasts with the fact that in many conflict managing situations, the well-being of the adversary is not the worker's prime concern. For instance, a social worker is not necessarily required to give priority to the psychiatrist's desire for his or her profession to be dominant in a work setting.

Another difference between the typical helping-type interaction and conflict managing situation is that in the former there is a tendency for the person seeking help to be in a somewhat dependent position vis-à-vis the helper. This is a common attribute of helping situations. Also, the helper is frequently "granted" authority based on expertise or position. However, a human service worker might be in for quite a shock if this "authority recognition" expectation was carried over to conflict situations. For instance, in the prior example, neither the social worker nor the psychiatrist would necessarily accept the greater authority of the other person in certain areas of decision making.

The motivations in entering conflict or helping situations also tend to differ. In conflict-type situations, the primary motivation may be the desire to gain an advantage in some arena, to defend one's interests, or to adhere to administrative-legal requirements. All of these motivations were present in one or the other of the two previously cited examples of conflict interactions. By way of contrast, the motivation in most helping situation is, virtually by definition, either to receive or to provide assistance of some sort, although this motivation may contain elements of ambivalence (e.g., wants help but fears incurring an obligation). Naturally, the intensity and enthusiasm attached to the motivation, even in helping interactions, may vary greatly from circumstance to circumstance.

There are also other social-psychological differences in conflict managing as compared with helping relationships. For instance, aggression and hostility, although not unknown by any means in helping situations, are more characteristic of conflict interactions. In addition, there tends to be more emphasis on "feeling" states in helping relationships. The adversaries in a conflict situation are much less inclined to focus on feelings than are the worker and client in a helping situation. Also, in helping interactions the worker is more likely to become involved in an intense "primary-type" relationship with the client. Although often equally intense, conflict relationships tend to be characterized by a more impersonal, task-centered quality.

Some roles performed by human service workers are more likely than others to involve conflict management activities. Although service providers and other members of organizations will all participate in professional conflict situations as part of their role responsibilities, there are some functional roles that have a particular connection with conflict managing activities. These include mediators, advocates, negotiators, social actionists, and similar roles. This is in contrast to the functional roles commonly linked to helping activities, for example, counselor, therapist, or provider of material assistance.

One implication, woven throughout all of the previous discussion, is that the fighting and helping functions, because of the decisive differences between them, require their own knowledge and skill repertoires—that is, their own sets of competencies. This is not to deny that the two functions also share an important common ground.

The responsibilities of most workers require the ability to engage in both types of activities. And this means that they should not only have a sufficiently broad range of knowledge and skills to cope with both functions, but that they should be able correctly to determine which competencies are called for in what circumstances. It may be equally undesirable to help when we should fight as to fight when we should help.

PROFESSIONAL/PERSONAL VALUES
AND CONFLICT MANAGEMENT

The fact that the ethical codes of most of the "helping professions" hardly address themselves to conflict-of-interest situations of the type discussed in this book is indicative of the extent of neglect of this subject by these occupations. This "gap" is particularly important since ethical issues arise with particular intensity in conflictual situations. And there is little in the way of professional guidance to assist workers in coping with them. A further complicating consideration is that in many circumstances of conflict, issues of personal values are sharply evoked.

An example of a general value stance that has a direct bearing on various conflict situations is the belief in the right to "self-defense" in coping with a ruthless opponent. Obviously, one's position on this value, and to the related one of "turning the other cheek," may greatly influence behavior in a conflict situation.

A more specific ethical question centering on this value problem, in a conflict transaction, is how one should respond to the use of "dirty tricks" by an adversary. Should such means be reciprocally employed by the human service worker if important and justifiable interests (such as the basic well-being of a client group) are threatened? What is the professionally responsible action in such a situation? And how does this relate to the worker's own profound values?

Ethics refers to standards of conduct that we set for ourselves, or that are defined for us by others, such as a professional association. *Dirty tricks* refers to various types of unethical actions. So the issue being raised is whether we are justified, in given circumstances, in responding to unethical or illegitimate actions on the part of others by similar means. For instance, if you work in an organization that discriminates against a category of persons, and if all normal efforts to change the situation have failed, are you justified in "leaking" information to the press or to an activist civil rights group? Or is a faculty member justified in "feeding" confidential information about faculty strategy to student leaders when he or she is unable to deter most of the academic staff from plans to deprive the students of what that faculty member and the students consider to be legitimate student "rights"?

In one case I know of, several very respected human service workers (psychologists and social workers) were prepared to destroy client files rather than permit them to be seized by governmental officials who were on a political "witch-hunt." This situation developed during the infamous McCarthy era. An even more extreme example is a "hostage" situation involving terrorists. Would it be justifiable for the human service worker who was doing the negotiating to break the agreement that was reached once the hostages had been released? After all, a contractual arrangement is invalid if agreed to under duress. These ethical problems do arise: I had the experience of being requested to pay a bribe, via a representative of the organization for which I was working, in order to get my personal belongings put on a ship at the time I was being evacuated in a siege situation.

Our position on this complex issue is that under certain circumstances the reactive use of undesirable means, such as dirty tricks, is justified. Among the determining criteria would be the importance and nature of the consequences of responding, or not responding, in like manner; the possibility or impracticality of reasonably effective alternative means; and the benefits and costs, including possible corruption of desirable ends by undesirable means. After all, means and ends are closely intertwined and have a continuous interacting impact on one another.

It is true, of course, that to justify the means by the end is dangerous, but to argue that this is never warranted is not only totally unrealistic but may even result in extreme social or personal harm. One of the assumptions underlying these comments is that dirty tricks will be used only in self- (or group) defense by the human service worker, and that the use will be as limited, in extent and severity, as possible.

In a later part of the book, such ethically problematic strategies and tactics as "manipulation" and "disadvantaging" are discussed.

Clearly, work related conflict situations involve the human service worker in a thicket of professional and personal value/ethical issues.

SUMMARY

We started this introductory chapter by taking the position that conflict management is an occupational necessity for human service workers. The area of conflict management that was staked out for attention is that concerned with conflicts of interest and commitment. We then defined *social conflict* and *interests, and clarified the meaning of false consciousness/pseudo-interests.* In turn, *self-interest* and *selfishness* were differentiated. This was followed by an explanation of the use of the term *commitment,* including the subcategory of *values.* The relationship between interests and commitment was also highlighted.

We stressed the importance for the human service worker of both the fighting and helping functions. In so doing we identified the distinctive characteristics of each type of activity, and put forth the argument that the "complete" human service worker needs to have command of the different knowledge and skills required for the effective implementation of each of these basic functions.

The chapter concluded with a discussion of professional and personal value/ethical issues and problems associated with conflict management.

NOTES

1. Although our definition is not identical with that of Lewis Coser (1956, p. 8), it has been greatly influenced by his formulation. For an interesting "sampling" of definitions see, Himes (1980, pp. 12-15).

2. For a very brief discussion of false consciousness, see *Encyclopedia of Sociology* (1974, pp. 106-107) and Kriesberg (1982, pp. 4-5).

3. For a concise discussion of the various meanings of *interest,* see Gould and Kolb (1964, pp. 343-344).

4. For a related use of the concept "instrumental," see Bennis, Benne, and Chen (1973).

Chapter 2

A PORTRAIT OF CONFLICT

Why the conflict, who is doing what to whom, and why does the prospect of engaging in conflict often give one a pain in the gut? These and similar questions arise as one is propelled into conflict situations.

The causes of any specific conflict consist of a unique cluster of factors and events, yet a number of "causal" categories do help to explain the origins of most conflicts. Please remember that these categories are not intended to be mutually exclusive. They are ways of bringing ideas together, rather than ways of compartmentalizing that which, in real situations, is often a complex amalgam.

THE BASES OF CONFLICT

BIOSOCIAL SOURCES

The prevalence of conflict has made it attractive to seek out its causes in the "nature of the beast." Instincts, hormones, the need for tension release, and the purportedly genetic-based "territorial imperative" have all been suggested (Himes, 1980, pp. 28-30; Kriesberg, 1982, pp. 24-26). Although it is reasonable to contend that there is a "built-in" potential in human beings for conflict (as there is for cooperation), this does not really explain very much. "Human nature" does not provide us with answers as to why conflicts do or do not develop over given issues, at specific times, and with certain characteristics. However, there are some "explanatory models" that combine various biosocial factors into a more promising framework. Often they are framed in terms of "frustration-aggression" constructs.

Frustration-aggression theories lie at the nexus of biological, psychological, and social explanations. At the most basic level—frustration, under given circumstances, results in aggression, hence conflict—there appears to be an important kernel of truth; yet in this form it is much more descriptive than explanatory. However, there is a useful "spin-off" formulation that advances our understanding of certain types of conflict. This is the concept of "relative deprivation" and the related notion of frustration produced by the tendency for expectations to increase more sharply than improvement in circumstances (or constant expectations and worsened conditions).

This concept helps us understand why disturbances in prisons often explode when reforms are already underway or why many of the academic departments that experienced the most acute student unrest during the 1960s and 1970s were those that had already made progressive changes.

PERSONALITY AND INTERACTIONAL SOURCES

We are all familiar with "difficult" people—those whose personalities are abrasive or whose patterns of interaction are conducive to conflict. In some cases the personality factors are deeply rooted or represent significant psychological disturbances. In other instances, the difficulties may be due to a lack of interpersonal skills and sensitivity. In addition, we know that some people just "rub each other the wrong way." We have all heard the phrase, when speaking of two people who can't get along, that the "chemistry is wrong." What we have in these situations, in addition to the factors previously mentioned, are such considerations as rivalry, inequities in exchange relationships, liking and disliking, the triggering of particular vulnerabilities, attempts to dominate, and even the loudness or quality of one's laughter.

Still another factor of considerable importance may be differences in interactional styles. In this connection, I can remember an occasion some years ago when, during a discussion in which there appeared to be a "controlled" difference of views, the other party suddenly "exploded" with considerable anger and told me to "get off the analytical horse and onto the intuitional ball." Obviously, two different intellectual/interactional styles weren't meshing.

It is readily apparent that personality factors and interactional styles play an important part in many conflictual situations. These social-psychological dynamics interact with organizational and structural elements, thus providing the complex contexts in which much conflict occurs.

STRUCTURAL SOURCES

Many conflicts are rooted in the structures of societies and organizations. A highly significant causal structural factor in conflict is the actual or perceived inequity in the distribution of material and nonmaterial advantages and rewards. Class, status, and power differentials are clearly the driving forces in many of the most important forms of conflict. An important addition to the classical analyses of these factors by Marx and Weber is the more recent work by Dahrendorf (1959), which focuses on the complex dynamics by which the social "categories" of differential rank, power, and interests develop into oppositional groups.[1] Gender and generational conflicts are also examples of the emergence of such oppositional groups.

Another source of conflict, within both overall social systems and more limited organizations, is the clash that develops between parts of systems that are incompatible, inconsistent, or poorly integrated. Related to such social strain is the tension produced by perceived gaps between the "real" and the "ideal" in the structuring of social relationships (Himes, 1980, pp. 31, 41).

We have all encountered conflicts rooted in structural conditions. The struggles associated with the civil rights and welfare rights movements, and the almost daily battles by nurses, social workers, and so forth, in health settings against domination by the medical profession are instances of structural conflict. So too is the struggle for changes in the legal treatment of rape victims.

These examples illustrate the great importance of structural sources of conflict.

CULTURAL AND IDEOLOGICAL
SOURCES OF CONFLICT

The clash of cultures is a phenomenon known to all of us. The conflicts faced by many children of migrants in trying to balance loyalty to their parents' cultural roots while striving to become part of a new culture are well known to all human service workers. And who can be unaware of the intense conflicts in our time based on sharp differences in political, social, and religious beliefs? Or of the disputes between individuals over deeply held conflicting values, such as those centering about the issues of abortion or sexual lifestyles? Clearly, then, the cultural and the ideological are other important areas of conflict.

CONVERGENCE

In the everyday world of work we frequently encounter a convergence of these various sources of conflict. Let's return to our earlier hypothetical example of the social worker who is in conflict with the team leader, a psychiatrist, over the issue of wanting more of a say in the decision-making process in regard to the treatment clients should receive. The unwillingness of the psychiatrist to relinquish any decision-making authority may result in the social worker feeling frustrated and reacting aggressively (biosocial sources). In addition, it is not too far-fetched to speculate that their personalities and interactional styles might be different, with the more domineering approach of the psychiatrist generating hostility in the social worker (personality and interactional sources).

As we shall mention later, disliking tends to promote disagreement, with a deteriorating, spiraling effect of the two factors. Of course, the basic framework of the conflict really derives from the differential position of the social worker and the psychiatrist, and of the professions of which they are members (structural source). This built-in inequality is likely to spark a conflict since workers in organizations frequently seek autonomy, influence, and prestige (Brager & Holloway, 1978, pp. 82-85). Finally, the beliefs of the social worker and the psychiatrist might differ as to the importance of "democratic" decision making in multidisciplinary teams (cultural/ideological source).

In this all too probable case of a conflict it is easy to see the underlying multiple sources. A similar convergence of dynamics often occurs in concrete conflictual situations. However, the fact that there are varied forces at work doesn't necessarily mean that they are of equal causal importance. For instance, in our previous example, if the structural "problem" of the inequality of the participants and their occupations did not exist, then the other conflict sources might have diminished greatly (or disappeared). This differential impact of sources should be taken into account in the decisions one makes as to how to prevent or manage conflicts.

TYPES OF CONFLICT

We have indicated that our primary focus will be on conflicts in which there is a genuine clash of opposing interests and commitment (e.g., the social worker-psychiatrist conflict example). However, there are other types of conflicts which may mimic, or get entangled with, authentic conflicts of interest/commitment. It is important to disentangle these "pretenders" from the real thing if we are to make appropriate strategic and tactical decisions. The following is a brief discussion of these other types of conflicts, as shown in Chart 2.1.

CHART 2.1
Types of Conflict

Type	Defining Characteristic
Interest/commitment conflicts	conflicts characterized by a genuine clash of opposing interests or commitments
Induced conflicts	conflicts intentionally created in order to achieve other than explicit objectives
Misattributed conflicts	conflicts involving incorrect attribution as to the behaviors, participants, issues, or causes
Illusionary conflicts	conflicts based on misperceptions or misunderstandings
Displaced conflicts	conflicts in which the opposition or antagnoism is directed toward persons or concerns other than the actual offending parties or the real issues
Expressive conflicts	conflicts characterized by a desire to express hostility, antagonism, or other strong feelings

INDUCED CONFLICT

Although an induced conflict is usually formulated as if it represents a genuine clash over divergent interests or commitments, it is, in fact, intentionally created in order to achieve other objectives. An example of such an induced conflict would be when the leader of a group generates intense conflict primarily as a way of gaining support from the membership, rather than to resolve divergent interests.

MISATTRIBUTED CONFLICT

This type of conflict involves misdirection, that is, the conflict may be between the wrong parties, over the wrong issues, or based on an erroneous assumption as to basic causes. For instance, a parent may accuse the wrong member of the family of having put a dent in the door of the new car. Or employees may blame an administrator for lack of resources when, in fact, the board of management was responsible, over the objections of the administrator. However, misattributed conflict is not always the result of individual errors in attribution. Stereotypes and ideological biases may also serve as generalized grounds for misattribution. For instance, antagonism may focus on the members of an ethnic group, toward which there is a negative stereotype, for being lazy and not wishing to work, when in reality the responsibility for the situation rests with a lack of employment opportunities and discriminatory hiring practices. In such situations, "self-fulfilling prophecies" may be vital in perpetuating misattributed conflicts. The distortions involved in misattributed conflict may be deliberately fostered, the consequence of "honest errors," or due to a lack of accurate information.

ILLUSIONARY CONFLICT

Illusionary conflicts are "false" conflicts in the sense that the claimed objective basis for them does not exist. Such conflicts may be due to misperceptions or misunderstandings. One common source of this type of conflict is difficulties in communications. We have all attended meetings at which two people go at each other in a spirited manner without realizing that they actually are in agreement. Of course, as in the case of misattributed conflict, the cause of illusionary conflict may be less benevolent than simply not having heard or understood what another person said or implied. False rumors, based on malevolence, may be circulated within an organization in order to provoke conflict. This may be due to personal dislike or a psychological disturbance (e.g., psychopathic behavior), or it might be part of a calculated "divide-and-conquer" strategy. In the latter instance, illusionary and misattributed conflict may almost blend into one another.

DISPLACED CONFLICT

In displaced conflict, opposition or antagonism is directed toward a person or concern other than the actual offending party or the real issue (Deutsch, 1977, p. 14). For instance, we may be angry at the "boss," but discretion prevails and we take it out on our spouse when we get home. Or we are upset by what we believe to be a lack of equity in a love relationship, but since this is too delicate or dangerous an issue to confront directly, we keep complaining that the other party is "thoughtless." Although there may be an overlap between this form of conflict and misattributed conflict, the emphasis in displaced conflict is less on misperception or misinformation and more on the intentional or "unconscious" directing of antagonism/opposition into safer, or more acceptable, channels.

EXPRESSIVE CONFLICT

Expressive conflict is characterized by a desire to express hostility and antagonism, that is, to release tension as a catharsis, or for other personalistic/psychological reasons (Olsen, 1968, p. 135). Such conflicts often appear, on the surface, to be interest- or issue-oriented, but the motivation may actually be quite different. We have all experienced, or at least observed, situations in which there was disappointment on the part of one person when the other party wouldn't "tango" (in the sense of refusing to join the conflict), with a resultant frustration for the person who came to fight. One complicating aspect of this type of conflict is that it may emerge from other types of conflict situations. For instance, the flow of adrenalin that was stimulated by a conflict over interests may keep the participants "hyped up," even after the basic problem is resolved, with a consequent residual desire to engage in expressive combat.

As has been demonstrated, conflicts have many sources, are of various types, and take a variety of forms. The correct "diagnosis" of conflicts is as important as is diagnosis in interpersonal "helping" relationships. Strategies, tactics, and techniques vary with the source and characteristics of the conflict; hence an incorrect "diagnosis" may lead to a nonproductive or even tragic outcome.

A serious error in understanding and coping with conflict, to which members of human service occupations are particularly prone, is the confusion of genuine conflicts of interest/commitment with expressive conflict (or even emotional problems). An example is that of the supervisor or administrator who counters an "objective" complaint by an employee about working conditions by defining the source of the objection as an internalized antagonism toward authority figures. Another illustration is that of the instructor who treats a serious intellectual disagreement by a student as a form of immature "heckling." Of course, the reverse can occur as well; that is, the participants may treat an expressive conflict as a true conflict of interests/commitment and then be thoroughly confused as to why a reasonable "solution" didn't resolve the difficulty.

The following Action Guide offers clues that may be useful in the diagnosis of conflict types.

Action Guide!

If one of the participants in an apparent conflict-of-interest situation pays little attention to genuine offers advanced by the other party, while engaging in increasingly aggressive verbal behavior, consider the possibility that there is a significant element of "expressive" conflict in the interaction.

If one or both of the parties in a public negotiating session take what appears to be an unrealistically "hard line" while obviously "playing" to constituents in the audience, consider the possibility of "induced" conflict. This cue is reinforced if, in private, informal conversations, the interaction is much more accommodating and receptive.

THE HUMAN FACE OF CONFLICT

In one sense, of course, everything about conflict is part of its "human face." However, in this section we are concerned with those personal and social-psychological characteristics of conflict that give it such an affective impact.

THE PASSION, THE PAIN, AND THE PLEASURE

One of the common characteristics of conflict is the arousal of strong emotions. This fact accounts in large part for the passion, pain, and pleasure associated with conflict processes. Most people have probably felt, during "combat," the emotions of anxiety, anger, fear, aggressiveness, and, perhaps, even exhilaration. No wonder that conflict may, on the one hand, be exhausting, while, on the other, it may produce a "high" for some combatants.

The tendency of "fighting" to call forth strong emotions helps to explain both the apprehension that conflict situations often induces in potential participants and the characteristics of such engagements. One such attribute of conflict is the rapidity with which it tends to escalate. We all know from personal experience that conflicts can rather quickly get "out of hand." Sometimes a small issue may suddenly blow up into a major crisis and we are left wondering what happened. This tendency toward rapidly increasing intensity and seriousness contributes to the discomfort often felt when confronted by a conflict situation. In the back of our minds there is the worry that the clash may get out of control.

Why does conflict tend to escalate in such a striking and often frightening fashion? One reason is that issue disagreement can be quickly converted into personal hostility. Another is the desire to protect oneself from attack, which frequently results in a defensiveness that may stimulate further conflict. Also, communications during conflictual situations tend to become distorted or "impoverished." In addition, anger and hostility, which often accompany conflict, aggravate the situation by making the participants less willing (or able) to think of new solutions, or even to compromise existing positions. Finally, there is, typically, an intensification of the "we-they" dichotomy that, in turn, promotes further conflict.

Conflicts originating in anger or personal dislike are usually more difficult to resolve in an effective and cooperative manner than those clashes revolving around differing desires. One reason for this is that there is a tendency for liking and agreement to reinforce each other, with the reverse being equally true (Freedman, Carlsmith, & Sears, 1970). Furthermore, the emotional stress associated with conflict in situations of high intensity may lead to perceptual and cognitive distortions (Deutsch, 1977, pp. 352-355).

Although the presence of intense emotions may interfere with effective problem-solving, a strong affective element in a dispute may provide the necessary emotional sustenance required to "fight the good fight."

For human service workers there are certain additional factors that may add to the discomforts that characterize conflict. For instance, people usually enter the human service occupations because of a desire to "help," rather than being indifferent to the "hurt" suffered by people. And, for many human service workers, engaging in conflict may be perceived of in "hurting or being hurt" terms. There may also be personality factors (e.g., compliance) that tend to work against involvement in conflict. In addition, some studies suggest that human service workers are likely to have less interest in domination/power than persons in other occupations. (See, for example, Rosenberg, 1957, chaps. 3, 4.) Furthermore, the gratification sought by many in the human service occupations in exchange for helping is that of being appreciated and liked. These are not the "exchanges" most frequently forthcoming in conflict situations.

The education and training of human service workers is another contributing factor. In some occupations, such as law, conflict is "bred" into neophytes throughout their professional education. This is in marked contrast to the educational orientation of most human service programs.

There is also, in all likelihood, a gender factor. Women make up a significant proportion of the membership of the human service occupations (a clear or overwhelming majority in some of them). The socialization patterns of many societies tend to discourage women from engaging in direct and overt conflict, particularly of a "public" type. This is reflected, in turn, in characteristic power and conflict orientations and styles, such as a greater preference by women for *indirect* modes of power, in comparison to men, who rely more on expertise, formal authority, and direct informational power (Raven, Centers, & Rodrigues, 1975, p. 232).

Whatever their personal inclinations, though, human service workers have no responsible choice but to engage in appropriate work-related conflicts. And this book is based on the assumption that the necessary competencies can be acquired—without undue trauma. As a matter of fact, it may even provide a certain amount of satisfaction and pleasure.

Pause for Reflection

Do you try to avoid professional conflict situations? If so, why? Try to think of specific examples. What tend to be your most characteristic "gut feelings" during work-related conflict situations? What are your most typical emotional reactions after you have been successful in a professional conflict? And after unsuccessful conflict engagements?

CONFLICT VARIABLES

THE ISSUES

The issues over which conflicts rage may be thought of as being analogous to the plot of a drama. In the same way that a plot provides the substance for and shapes the drama, so too the issues underlying a given conflict decisively influence the nature of that struggle.

The issues around which conflicts frequently emerge are the different interests of those who may become contestants or combatants. Interests vary in substance, intensity, and significance. Some of the issues over which people clash are of utmost importance, while others appear (at least to an outside observer, if not to the parties in the conflict) trivial in the extreme. The ramifications of the issues in dispute may affect the lives of millions of people, or just have "gut meaning" to the immediate participants.

Among the ways in which the issues at the root of conflicts vary are degree of generality or specificity, linkages with other issues, historic antecedents, and the rigidity of the positions expressing these issues. In addition, some issue struggles are seen by the adversaries as being accessible to "rule-regulated" conflict management strategies (e.g., negotiation), while others may be defined in terms of total victory or defeat—or a continuing impasse. The substance of a conflict—that is, the issues—and the process of managing the conflict are interactive.

Examples of potential conflict issues in the human services include such policy and organizational matters as the criteria for client eligibility for services, management decision-making styles, and, at the personal level, the question of which worker should have which office.

THE PHYSICAL SETTING

The physical milieu within which conflict takes place can have a considerable influence on the course and management of a conflict. Not only do the physical arrangements of rooms and buildings have a powerful impact in their own right, they also combine with differences in status, role, interactional style, and personality to influence behavior in conflict situations (Whyte, 1978, p. 373).

Important functions of the physical milieu (Steele, 1973, pp. 439-447) include the following:

(a) security and shelter
(b) facilitation of social contact
(c) symbolic meaning (e.g., status differentials)
(d) task facilitation (e.g., appropriate facilities and layouts)
(e) comfort and pleasure
(f) territorial designation (e.g., who is the "host" and who is the "guest")

Other related factors that may have an influence on conflicts, particularly those involving cultural clashes, include such matters as differences between people (and peoples) in attitudes toward privacy, closeness or distance in interaction, loudness of voice, and the general use of space.

A consideration of particular relevance in conflict management is site location. In their discussion of the significance of site selection in bargaining situations, Rubin and Brown (1975, p. 85), citing various research studies, contend not only that bargaining on one's home territory is likely to increase assertiveness, but even that the "territory on which bargainers find themselves is likely to have a far greater influence on their level of assertiveness than more stable personality characteristics."

The study of the significance of setting for conflict management is still in its early days, but present indications are that it is an area of considerable importance.

Pause for Reflection

How would you arrange a room that is to be a setting for a conflictual meeting so as to (1) maximize direct confrontation between the participants, (2) minimize direct confrontation between the participants, (3) stress status differences among the participants, (4) emphasize equality among the participants, and/or (5) discourage the monopolization of a discussion by two of the adversaries.

THE PARTICIPANTS

The parties to a conflict may be individuals, groups or other social categories, organizations, or inclusive systems such as nations. However, even when large units are involved, individuals represent them in the conflict management processes. The participants in a conflict, singly or collectively, may be characterized as follows: the contenders, the constituents, the potential partisans, the audience, and third parties. Together they may be thought of as the cast of characters in a conflictual encounter, although not all of them necessarily will be present in every conflict situation.

The *contender* is the individual participant, or group of participants, directly participating in the conflict management situation.[2] In our earlier example of the social worker-psychiatrist at odds with each other over the former's desire to have more of a say in the decision-making process, both of them would be contenders. It is the contenders who "act out" the conflict management strategies and tactics—although they may be formally or informally representing other persons, these other persons being the *constituents* of the contenders. For instance, in the above illustration, the other social workers in the agency may be the constituents of the social worker who is directly involved in the dispute. This depends on whether the social worker is simply acting as an individual or is representing the agency or profession. This is true for the psychiatrist as well.

Gamson (1968, p. 32) defines *potential partisans* as those "who, for a given decision, are affected by the outcome in some 'significant' way." He goes on to say that they "need not perceive the significance of the decision for themselves or have either the inclination or the ability to influence the outcome if they do perceive it." However, it "will make some difference in the lives of these potential partisans if one thing rather than another is decided." These potential partisans may be individuals as well as groups. In the social worker-psychiatrist imbroglio, for instance, the psychologists in the agency could be *potential partisans*, since their decision-making role in the agency might be enhanced if the social worker's goal in the conflict is attained.

The term *audience* refers to those persons who are "present," physically or psychologically, at the site of the conflict management interaction.

Psychological presence pertains when it is supposed by a bargainer that, even though the proceedings may not actually be witnessed, the events that transpire and the performance of the bargainers will eventually become known to an audience.

An audience, moreover, may be either dependent or nondependent on a bargainer for its outcomes, and dependency may apply either to tangible outcomes . . . or intangible ones. (Rubin & Brown, 1975, p. 73)

Audiences may be composed of *constituents, potential partisans*, or just interested but uninvolved *observers*. In our social worker-psychiatrist example, even if the social worker was just acting as an individual *contender* (not representing social workers as such), the other social workers in the agency might still be an audience for the unfolding conflict. And, as we shall see in the chapters on negotiations, audiences may well influence the process of conflict management.

In some conflict situations, *third parties* are called upon to assist in the process. Conciliators, mediators, arbitrators, or judges may play the parts of third parties. The role of third parties in disputes will be elaborated later in the book.

The performances of the actors in the conflict management encounter is influenced by their personalities. After all, no two persons enact a role in exactly the same way, not even when it is carefully scripted. However, it is difficult, except in extreme cases, to gauge the importance of these factors relative to structural and situational elements. Clearly, the significance of such considerations will vary with the nature of the conflict and the participants. All of us are familiar with situations in which interaction became conflictual because of the moods, temper, hostility, aggressiveness, or impatience of one or more of the participants. And this outcome is even more striking if one of the parties is a highly disturbed person. What is difficult to ascertain, though, is the overall relationship between personality characteristics, as such, and conflict behavior.

After acknowledging the limitations in our present knowledge and the difficulties confronting research in this area, Terhune (1970, pp. 217, 229-230) hypothesized that conflict is more likely when one or more of the participants is "rigid" (e.g., authoritarian) and generally mistrustful. He also believes that present evidence suggests that there may be differences in the conflict behavior of certain population groups, such as men and women. One particular difficulty is untangling motives from strategies/tactics in actual conflict situations since participants may deliberately employ various devices to mask their preferred styles or modes of conflict management (McClintock, 1977, p. 75). For instance, a usually aggressive person may adopt a charming, reasonable, "laid back" style as a conflict tactic.

Certain types of conflicts (i.e., misattributed and illusionary) are characterized by errors in perception and interpretation. This suggests that personal cognitive factors can contribute significantly to the emergence of conflicts, as well as to their management. One study found, for example, that it is reasonably common for the adversaries to draw incorrect inferences as to how important their opponents consider various issues (Brehmer & Hammond, 1977, pp. 92, 97).

Such cognitive factors as abstractness-concreteness, tolerance of ambiguity, and dogmatism may well influence tendencies toward cooperation or conflict. Driver (cited in Terhune, 1970, p. 209) found that groupings composed of concrete-minded persons were prone to aggressiveness. He concluded that this was because, under stress, the cognitive characteristic of concreteness resulted in "perceptual simplification"—with a tendency toward hostile and suspicious attitudes, coupled with the elimination of nonaggressive responses as a perceived alternative.

Although personal factors are clearly implicated in conflict behavior, much more research is necessary before firm conclusions can be advanced with confidence. In part, this is because personal characteristics do not exist in isolation: They need to be seen in terms of a dynamic interchange involving other persons and their interactive responses, the situation, and the context.

CONFLICT RESOURCES AND THEIR USE

The participants in a conflictual situation possess a range of conflict-relevant resources—in effect, all the means and commodities available to them that might be activated toward achievement goals or desired outcomes. And these resources are expressed through the processes of conflict engagement. The two most important resources may be *influence* and *power*. Both may also be thought of as processes that require drawing on other resources. We'll explain.

Unfortunately, these terms are often unclear, lacking in agreed-upon meanings (Gamson, 1968, p. 59). For our purposes, we'll define these terms on the basis of potential utility and minimal confusion, while taking into account popular meanings and various technical arguments.

We will begin by distinguishing between *influence* and *power*, even though in some situations they may be so intermeshed as to be virtually indivisible.[3] For example, both tend to refer to the potential possessed by individuals, groups, organizations, or larger social systems to bring about a desired outcome, through impact on other parties. Sometimes, in reference to power, stronger language is used, such as the ability to impose one's will over opposition. Influence and power also share the characteristic of being social processes rather than static attributes. For instance, if you are on an island without anyone else present, you will not be in a position to exercise influence or power, at least not in respect to other human beings. Further, both terms suggest the likelihood of at least a partially unequal relationship, although in some instances there may be a reciprocal power or influence system of a basically balanced type.

Power, when compared with influence, suggests a greater potential (and, perhaps, willingness) to overcome serious obstacles and resistances by means of strong measures, some of which may be subtly or blatantly coercive. There is also a greater sense of negative sanctions associated with the concept of power than with influence. Influence, in turn, seems to imply more emphasis on affecting outcomes by means of convincing or persuading. There is, additionally, the suggestion that influence depends on ultimate agreement by those subject to it. Further, influence is often exercised in an informal, personal, or indirect manner.[4] It is also more likely than is power to be exercised "unintentionally." Because of these differences, even if primarily a matter of degree and emphasis, it is desirable to differentiate between the two concepts.

In the exercise of both influence and power, there may be many a slip between the intention and the outcome, and even the actual causal relationship may be quite unclear in some instances. This latter point is neatly, and amusingly, made in a story told by Gamson (1968, p. 60):

> A man who, early each morning, enthusiastically threw bits of newspaper in the street. One morning, a woman who had watched this performance for several months approached him and asked him what he was doing. "I'm throwing this paper down to keep the elephants out of the streets," he replied. "But there are no elephants in the streets," she reproached him. "That's right," he said, triumphantly, "effective, isn't it?"

The concept of authority usually refers to the power that inheres in a position (e.g., executive of an organization). The occupant derives power from the role and regulations associated with the position itself. This is what is implied in the military saying that when you salute a superior officer you are saluting the position, not the person. Since the source of such authority resides in an "authorized" position, it is often said that such authority is "legitimated power," which is exercised with the concurrence of those subject to it.

There is another, very different type of authority in which the legitimacy of the leader, in the eyes of his or her followers, derives from the "extraordinary" qualities of the person—qualities which are, in a sense, self-validating. It is thought to be obligatory for those who recognize such qualities in their leaders to offer them total devotion and trust. Weber referred to this phenomenon as "charismatic authority," and contrasted it with rational and traditional authority (Parsons, 1947, pp. 358-363). The leadership in Iran right after the revolution is a striking example of charismatic authority in operation—an example, some might even say, of charismatic authority run amuck.

Some writers on the subject treat power as the potential for employing sanctions and force as the exercise of such power (Tedeschi, 1972, p. 7).

However, we prefer Himes's (1980, pp. 79-85) formulation: He describes the power potential as residing in resources (power resources) that, in order to be exercised, must be mobilized, delivered, and injected into given social situations, and then properly "managed" in order to accomplish the desired objectives. It is active power that gains one's will, overcomes resistance, influences people, and causes behavioral change.

The transformation of latent power into active power through mobilizing resources requires, as a first step, the identification of those resources. All too often people underestimate their capacities to mobilize, effectively deploy, and manage the resources so as to be effective in conflict situations. This is particularly true of individuals and groups who do not possess highly visible and traditional power resources, such as control over money and jobs. As a consequence, many groups and individuals believe themselves to be more powerless than they really are. In our experience, human service workers often fall into this category. For instance, the capacity to force an administrator to invest time and effort (and to risk appearing ineffectual to higher-level executives) in dealing with repetitive and well-organized complaints may be an unrealized power resource of considerable potentiality for "line" workers (and clients) in many human service organizations.

Among the more commonly recognized conflict resources are physical coercion; money; control of communication, organizational support, and numbers; authority; the right to reward or punish; control over goods and services; the ability effectively to withhold one's labor; leadership; and possession of necessary but scarce skills. Less frequently identified are such power/influence resources as time, energy, imagination, knowledge, communication skills, the opportunity to "rock the boat" (thus creating stress and embarrassment for superordinates), co-optation of a consultant, attractiveness, the obligation created by a nonreciprocated social exchange, an imposing physical presence and skill in presentation of self, patience, controlled intensity, "helplessness," the inducing of guilt, the evoking of moral commitments, reputation, potential alliances, control of the physical environment, analytical skills, emotional and physical "staying power" (e.g., "posterior endurance"), self-discipline, and even simulated anger, irrationality, and desperation.

Power and influence resources, such as those mentioned above, might be classified under the following headings:[5]

(1) *coercive*—the capacity to "punish," to deprive, to frustrate, and to raise "costs" to an unacceptable level
(2) *reward*—the capacity for providing others with something they want or need (i.e., benefits)

(3) *expert*—the capacity to provide others with special skills and abilities. There is also the implication that the expert could withhold expertise, thus creating a type of "withholding" power.

(4) *positional*—the authority derived from filling an "official" position; hence the "legitimated" power residing in the role and prerogatives adhering to that position

(5) *informational*—the capacity to control (provide, restrict, channel) the flow of information, thus having the potential to provide advantages for some and to disadvantage others

(6) *exchange*—the potential to exact desired behaviors through the creation of an imbalance in exchange relationships, that is, creating a social or psychological debt by means of an unfulfilled obligation. "Calling in" a political "I.O.U." is an example of this power.

(7) *mobilizational*—the capacity to generate and mobilize other people's support for desired goals, hence increasing one's own potential clout

(8) *moral*—the capacity to gain given objectives by invoking moral commitments held by other persons, or creating guilt in them by making them morally responsible to provide support or assistance

(9) *personal power*—personal characteristics (e.g., attractiveness, persuasiveness, "charisma") that enable persons to affect the behavior of others in desired directions

Most of the previously enumerated specific power resources fall within one or the other of these categorical headings. Some of the categories have more application to power (e.g., coercion), while others are more related to influence (e.g., expertise). However, there is considerable overlap between the categories in this respect.

There are certain characteristics of power that one should keep in mind in order to be a success (or even a survivor) in conflict management situations. For instance, there is a well-known phrase, "a steel fist in a velvet glove." What this suggests is that power may be most effective when it is "hidden," or at least not too obvious. One reason for this is that the "naked" use of power is likely to create a reaction in the same sense that threats tend to produce like responses. Also, the masking of power often reduces other "costs" that are commonly associated with its direct application. Among the benefits (reduced costs) of obscuring the use of power are maintaining "good feelings"; reducing anger and avoiding the rupture of personal relationships; preventing the exposure of the "bluff" element that is frequently involved in certain uses of power; and maintaining support for the person or group in power. These advantages result from the fact that power often appears less arbitrary and more legitimate if masked. Even in "one-party" political systems, it is frequently deemed important to have "popular" elections, although there is only a single slate of candidates.

The manipulative use of masked power may be destructive and unethical. A case in point is counseling a student out of a program in such a way that the student appears to have made the decision, even though the faculty has already decided that the student will not be allowed to continue. Or giving a student association the apparent authority to make decisions pertaining to student affairs so long as it makes the "right decisions." Of course, the association, in this example, is not aware of the implicit reservation that it is permitted only to make the "correct" choices (as determined by the administrator). Another instance is the executive in an organization who "permits" the staff to make important policy decisions but stacks the key committees with surrogates to assure that the decisions are in harmony with his or her thinking.

The danger of the manipulative use of hidden power is that it may deceive people by obscuring the fact they are being subjected to coercive actions (justified or not). It may also hide the identity of the powerful person. Although masked power can be effective, at least in the short run, it may corrupt the processes of decision making and distort conflict management activities. My view is that it is important to know if someone is controlling your actions—and to know who that someone is. This is a requirement for effective and democratic decision making, and it is necessary in order to protect one's legitimate interests. However, the responsible use of power does not require that it be flaunted or that all one's cards have to be exposed.

A relatively widespread tendency of powerful and influential people is to try to extend that power/influence beyond legitimate and relevant areas. An example would be a person (e.g., a "professor of Romance Languages" or a "chest surgeon") who writes a letter to the local newspaper in reference to governmental policy on aid to the unemployed and signs the letter using the high (but irrelevant) occupational status designation. Or calling for a seat at the opera and using an impressive designation, such as professor or doctor. Even the use of M.D. or Ph.D. on one's checks may be designed to exert influence beyond one's arena of competence, or in an unsuitable manner. This misuse of power/influence can, unjustifiably, result in advantages and disadvantages for people.

A third characteristic of power and influence is that they represent potentialities that can be used for either prosocial or antisocial ends. We don't agree with those who consider power to be essentially a positive resource that can get desirable things done. Nor do we share the reverse view that power is inherently an instrument of oppression. We believe power/influence can be used for any end, good or bad, hence the goal is all important. Also, in view of the very real kernel of truth in the statement that "power corrupts," it is our conviction that proper mechanisms to lessen the likelihood of this happening are a necessity in any organization, including those providing human services.

Some key action implications, flowing from our discussion of power and influence, are highlighted in the following Action Guide.

Action Guide!

(1) Realistically assess your power/influences, and those of your adversary, before deciding to engage in conflict. Don't underestimate less obvious resources—they can be very effective.

(2) Remember, the flaunting or full disclosure of power resources may prove to be counterproductive. But resist the temptation to engage in the manipulative use of masked power—it may have very destructive consequences.

(3) Avoid overkill in the use of power. Overkill leads to squandering of resources and may provoke a dangerous backlash.

CONSTRUCTIVE AND DESTRUCTIVE OUTCOMES OF CONFLICT

The discussion, thus far, might have reinforced a commonly held view that conflict is essentially a destructive event. It is all too true that unnecessary or inappropriate conflict is unwise and sometimes tragic in its outcome. However, conflict can have benefits as well as costs. Among the potentially positive outcomes are necessary social changes (such as the attainment of a more just society); the development of a sense of solidarity among members of groups engaged in conflict; the emergence of creative ideas; the formulation of new policies, procedures, and services; the reformation and renewal of organizations and their programs; and heightened enthusiasm and purpose among the conflicting participants.

The possible negative consequences, which are more often recognized than are the benefits, include physical or psychological injury; interference with reasoned problem-solving; the rupture of social relationships; the escalation of differences into hardened antagonistic positions; increased hostility and misperceptions; and emotional exhaustion. Many other likely outcomes could have been included on both the benefit and the cost sides, but the above listing should convey an adequate sense of the possibilities.

SUMMARY

We opened this chapter with a discussion of the sources of conflict. Four categories of conflict "causes"—the biosocial, personality and interactional, structural, and cultural/ideological—were identified. It was observed that in real-life conflicts, there tends to be a "convergence" of various of these sources.

After reiterating the fact that the type of conflict we are primarily emphasizing in this volume is that concerned with interests and commitment, we briefly described other categories of conflict that sometimes mimic, or get entangled with, conflicts of interest and commitment. These are induced, misattributed, illusionary, displaced, and expressive types of conflict. It was noted that it is important to be able to disentangle these "pretenders" from genuine clashes of interest/commitment in order to make appropriate choices of strategies, tactics, and techniques.

Our attention then shifted to selected characteristics of conflictual situations, particularly the affective dimension. In discussing the "human face of conflict," we explored some of the reasons for the passion, pain, and pleasure that frequently accompanies conflict. Particular factors that tend to make it difficult for human service workers to be "willing" participants in conflict management situations were noted.

The next section was devoted to a discussion of the key conflict variables. These were identified as the issues, the physical setting, the participants, and conflict resources and their use.

The chapter concluded with a brief comment on constructive and destructive outcomes of conflict. Conflict, in some circumstances, may be useful and desirable, just as in other situations it may prove to be wasteful and harmful.

NOTES

1. For a brief review of these theories, see Himes (1980, pp. 30-32).

2. Charles Tilly (1978, p. 52) uses the term *contender,* although in a more specific sense than we do.

3. Some writers on the subject equate influence and power or consider one as a subcategory of the other. Others treat power as the potential capability to influence.

4. Although Himes (1980, p. 79) treats influence as a subcategory of power, he attributes personal and informal characteristics to it.

5. Categories 1, 2, 3, and 5 were suggested by French and Raven and appear in Raven et al. (1975, p. 219).

Chapter 3

A FRAMEWORK FOR CONFLICT MANAGEMENT

This chapter provides a framework for the analysis of conflict management and for engaging in the process itself. A brief recapitulation of some of the central ideas in the prior chapters will serve as the springboard for the depiction of the framework.

Early in the volume we pointed out that our primary concern would be with one type of conflict situation—that of conflicts of interests and commitment. It is important to keep this focus in mind. However, we also cautioned that other forms of conflict, namely, induced, misattributed, illusionary, displaced, and expressive, sometimes get mixed up, or confused, with disputes over interests/commitment. Remember, we are not including, within the purview of this book, "treatment" of a client's conflicts, nor will we zoom in on those conflictual aspects of the "interpersonal/helping" process that fall outside the realm of conflicts of interest and commitment. This is not because such matters are unimportant; rather, they provide the substance for a different book with a different mission.

We identified various sources of conflict, such as the biosocial, personality-interactional, structural, and cultural/ideological. The significance of these categories for conflict management is that the issues we center on in disputes, and the strategies and tactics we employ, should be related to the relevant conflict sources. For instance, if a conflict is primarily about the structure of decision making in a human service team (remember our social worker-psychiatrist example), we ought to direct our attention, resources, and strategic/tactical decisions toward dealing effectively with that arena. If we lose our bearings and accept an erroneous definition of the situation (e.g., the conflict is simply a matter of incompatible personalities), we may well find that we did not do a good job of conflict management. In fact, by obscuring the real issues (linked to the real causes) we may have made matters worse.

As we consider, in the next chapters, the selection of strategies and tactics and how to use them, keep in mind the previously identified categories of power resources. For example, if one is weak in "coercive resources," it might be well to stay away from using the "big stick" (threats/punishments) and rely more on the "carrot," if reward resources are available. On the other hand, if a person is poorly endowed in reward or coercive resources, the strategical/tactical maneuvers might be directed toward exploiting "moral resources" (assuming they are present) by "invoking a value commitment" to justice. Obviously, resources and strategies/tactics must go hand in hand.

A FRAMEWORK OF CONFLICT MANAGEMENT

In laying out the framework, we will first identify and describe categories of work-related conflict management interactions. This conceptual categorization is, we believe, preferable to the more usual way of describing and organizing professional behaviors according to a "macro/micro" dichotomy.

CATEGORIES OF
CONFLICT MANAGEMENT INTERACTIONS

Although many writers in the human services use the macro/micro (e.g., community work and helping/clinical, respectively) dichotomy as a way of describing and organizing professional behaviors, we find this approach essentially misleading and inadequate. Thus we shall use alternative conceptual categories throughout the book. This point is illustrated by our categorization of work-related "conflict management interactions." The categories are described and then depicted in Chart 3.1.

(1) *Interpersonal: one-on-one.* One often encounters personal conflicts on the job, many of which are specifically role-related. They may occur in two-person (dyadic) situations or in a larger group context. An example would be conflict between two colleagues due to differing and irritating interactional styles. Excluded from this designation are clinical-type relationships between worker and clients that focus on the "inner" conflicts experienced by clients.

CHART 3.1
Categories of Conflict Management Interactions

Category	Major Characteristics	Examples
Interpersonal: one-on-one	The conflict management interaction is between persons, each of whom is acting as an individual, in a work related but "nonhelping" capacity.	A paid worker and a volunteer are in conflict over role definitions.
		Two workers who are supposed to be cooperating find themselves in frequent conflict because of personal antagonism.
		Members of a human service team are in conflict as to the procedure for selecting/electing a leader.
		A worker charges an administrator with sexual harassment.
		A supervisor and worker clash over the latter's demand for more autonomy in decision making.
		Two workers in a case conference disagree as to the proper course of treatment for a client.
Interpersonal: representational	At least one of the parties in the conflict management interaction represents an organization or a constituent (a unit or a person).	The representatives of a secular social agency and a religious organization are in conflict over policies related to abortion.
		The workers in an agency (through their representative) threaten to go on strike unless their salaries and working conditions are improved.

(continued)

CHART 3.1 Continued

Category	Major Characteristics	Examples
		An "involuntary" client challenges the worker over the requirement that he or she report in regularly. In this situation the worker represents the court.
		The representative of a civil liberties organization that is opposed to religion in the schools engages in a public debate with a legislator who is in favor of allowing time for prayers in the public schools.
		The student association in a school of social work, through its representative, seeks more participation rights in regard to curricular decisions, against some faculty opposition.
		Representatives of two departments within the same organization are in conflict over the allocation of resources for their respective units.
Interpersonal: Third-party interventions	The human service worker, in a third-party role, facilitates the conflict management efforts of other persons.	An administrator intervenes to assist in the management of conflict between two department heads.
		A worker mediates in a divorce-linked dispute over child custody.

(continued)

(2) *Interpersonal: representational.* In many types of conflict situations the worker represents an organization, a group, or an individual client. The worker may be serving as an advocate, agent, or spokesperson. In this

CHART 3.1 Continued

Category	Major Characteristics	Examples
		A worker, acting as an ombudsman, is called upon to determine whether the charge of sex discriminination made by an employee is supported by the evidence.
		A worker instructs couples in conflict management techniques.
		A worker serves as a consultant to a self-help organization experiencing severe intragroup conflict, in an attempt to help the participants manage their disagreements more constructively.
		A worker, employed by a dispute resolution center, mediates in a conflict between two neighbors over the erecting of a fence between their houses.
Interpersonal: clinical	The "treatment" of clients experiencing social-psychological/emotional conflicts, either of an intrapersonal or interpersonal character.	A worker serves as a family therapist for a disturbed and conflicted family.

category, the worker is engaging in conflict management on behalf of a constituency, be it an organized unit of some sort (e.g., a student association, a welfare rights group) or another person.

(3) *Interpersonal: third-party intervention.* Human service workers may be called upon to serve in third-party roles, providing assistance in the management of a conflict. For instance, a worker may be called upon to serve as a mediator, as a conciliator, or even as an ombudsman. There may also be opportunities for instructing groups or individuals in conflict

CHART 3.2

Conflicts of Interest and Commitment: Modes of Conflict Management

Mode	Criteria for Use	Strategies	Key Tactics
Forestalling and sidestepping	conflict is unnecessary, inappropriate, or the costs would be too high	prevention avoidance	increased organizational responsiveness early identification of latent conflicts "hot lines" use of "institutionalized dissenters" exposure of differences prior to becoming conflicts diffusion of conflict managing skills denial flight relinquishment suspension
Generating conflict	nonconflictual means are ineffectual; power/influence resources are available; and the costs of conflict would not be unacceptably high	explicating latent conflicts and identifying areas in which conflictual actions would be desirable creating conflict managing capabilities	"consciousness-raising" exposing a false consensus providing opportunities for the articulation of significant differences identifying power/influences resources generating resources developing confidence in conflict management

Conflict management by covert means	inability or lack of desire to cope with overt conflict inability to get the other contender to engage in overt rule-structured conflict management lack of power parity exposes vulnerable contender to excessive risks/costs if overt conflict management is used	passive resistance or concealment manipulation	negativism noncompliance "stonewalling" deceit disadvantaging seduction emotional "extortion" divide and conquer
Conflict management by emergent agreement	one or more of the contenders is accessible to influence by the other(s) or to the introduction of new "objective" data both contenders are willing to engage in a search for "better" solutions situation is not defined as one of sharply opposed vital interests or cherished commitments anticipation that this mode will lead to more satisfactory outcome, with fewer costs, than other options	coactive disputation	joint problem-solving fact finding gentle persuasion consensual decision making
Conflict management by directly negotiated agreement	both contenders believe their objectives may best be gained by a negotiated mutual benefit agreement or a "give and take" solution	negotiation (substrategies: integrative and distributive)	definition of issues focusing on interests use of "objective" criteria (negotiating on "merit") inventing mutually beneficial "options"

(continued)

CHART 3.2 Continued

Mode	Criteria for Use	Strategies	Key Tactics
	the absence of extreme disparities in the balance of power between the contenders willingness to negotiate may be subsequent to the preliminary or costly/inconclusive use of other modes		bargaining subtactics: "give and take" (concessional exchange) "carrot and stick" debate
Conflict management by indirect or procedural means	inability or lack of desire on the part of the contenders to reach an agreement through direct transactions dissatisfaction with the results obtained from other modes of conflict management, or with prior decisions a willingness or requirement to submit conflictual issues to indirect mechanisms or procedural resolution	use of third parties use of "quasi-judicial" and judicial structures use of formalized decision-making procedures	mediation teaching conflict management competencies use of consultant use of an ombudsperson use of quasi-judicial and judicial "appeals structures" voting
Conflict management by exercise of authority or power	inability or lack of desire on the part of a contender with positional power to use other conflict managing modes	authoritative decision making exercise of superior power	persuasion bargaining *force majeure* enforcing rules setting limits "pocket veto" industrial action

managing skills. This instruction may have a preventive function as well as being a mode of conflict intervention.

(4) *Interpersonal: clinical.* Although we have included this category in our chart in order to recognize its place in the total picture, it will not be covered in this volume. The reason for this exclusion is that the provision of "clinical" services to clients suffering from "internalized" conflicts, or those conflicts associated primarily with the "disturbed" aspects of interpersonal relationships, is more properly included in a treatment-oriented book.

MODES OF CONFLICT MANAGEMENT

We now turn to the second major component of our framework, the modes of conflict management. These modes are depicted in Chart 3.2 and will be discussed in the forthcoming chapters. For each mode, key strategies and tactics are identified, as are the circumstances (criteria) likely to invoke their use. Please keep in mind the fact that in any given conflict situation the modes, and their correlated strategies and tactics, may overlap. And the same strategies and tactics might be employed in connection with different modes. This disclaimer does not imply that our chart is made up of arbitrary relationships. On the contrary, there is a clear conceptual and practical relationship among the modes, strategies, and tactics. But it is not an invariant linkage.

In many instances the strategies and tactics, which together we define here as modes of conflict management, overlap the previously described categories of relationships. Thus the same activities may be engaged in regardless of whether it's a one-on-one or representational relationship. However, some patterns are more typical than others. For example, in representational transactions, negotiations tend to be explicit and the agenda formalized. By contrast, in many one-on-one conflict management interactions the negotiations are implicit, and without benefit of a formal agenda. For instance, compare a worker-management negotiating session (representational) with the informal negotiations that go on between two workmates as they attempt to iron out their differences as to the holidays that each one will be required to work.

One-on-one conflict management relationships tend to be not only more informal, and implicit, than those of a representational type, but they are also more likely to have a pronounced emotional content (Argyle, 1983, pp. 149, 160-164). For this reason, when conflicts of interest/commitment are acted out through one-on-one relationships, they are particularly susceptible to becoming intermixed with other forms of conflict, such as expressive, displaced, or misattributed. Hence, they have a distinct potential for ending up with a scenario rather different from that which was intended or expected.

One other general characteristic of the modes of conflict management has to do with the "rules" governing them.[1] Some modes, and within them strategies and tactics, are more structured by explicit statements of expected (or required) behaviors than are others. For instance, in a conflict game such as football there are rule books. On the other hand, almost anything goes in a "street fight." However, when a supervisor and worker are in conflict they are likely to be guided by implicit norms of behavior (e.g., politeness). And the strategies of covert resistance and manipulation, depicted in the chart, tend to be less rule-regulated than is negotiation.

Rules are important because they indicate the appropriate ways in which to conduct conflict management activities, thus increasing predictability and making the costs of engaging in conflict more controllable. For rules to be effective and adhered to the following conditions should obtain:

(1) The rules must be clear.
(2) The rules must be fair (and appear to be fair), thus allowing each party a reasonable opportunity to pursue what they consider to be their legitimate interests without being unduly disadvantaged.
(3) The rules must be applied consistently.
(4) There must be mutual adherence to the rules.
(5) If the rules are not working in what appears to be an equitable manner, there should be appropriate, regularized procedures for modifying the rules.
(6) Depending on the nature and context of the conflict, there may need to be regularized appeal procedures.
(7) Violations of rules should be detectable and disapproval or other sanctions should be invoked by such violations.
(8) There must be supporting social norms.

No matter how rule-structured or issue oriented one's approach to a conflict situation may be, personal factors, such as liking and disliking, do enter into the process—sometimes decisively. It is a serious error to consider conflict management a technical rather than a human encounter. To avoid such a distortion in emphasis, keep in mind basic principles of constructive human interaction—principles that are of even more than ordinary importance in the tension-charged atmosphere that characterizes many conflicts. The Action Guide that follows casts certain of these principles in action terms.

Action Guide!

In conflict situations, remember to remember these basics of human relationships:

—Maintain fairness and objectivity.
—Don't criticize a participant in front of others.
—Don't be critical of the other relationships of your adversary.
—Don't attack your opponent's motives.
—Don't indicate "concern" or doubts about your adversary's emotional well-being.
—Don't attribute the divergent views of your opponent to personality or personal factors.
—Don't depreciate another participant behind his or her back.
—Reciprocate debts, favors, and compliments.
—Keep confidences.
—Demonstrate a caring concern and be emotionally supportive, even in respect to an adversary.
—Take into account your opponent's desire for recognition and self-esteem, and other matters of "face."
—Avoid blatant or subtle manifestations of arrogance.

STRATEGIES, TACTICS, AND TECHNIQUES: DEFINITIONS AND RELATIONSHIPS

We will conclude the presentation of the framework with a brief discussion of the meaning of some terms we have already used, namely, *strategy, tactics,* and *techniques.*

The term *strategy*, as used here, refers to an operational plan to achieve a conflict goal. It is a set of ideas that provides a framework for, and links together, more limited behaviors that constitute the *tactics.* "Strategy may thus be said to integrate a consideration regarding *what* to do about a problem with a concern regarding *how* to go about doing it" (Brager & Holloway, 1978, p. 131).

A *tactic* is a specific implementing maneuver that frequently involves the mobilizing and exercise of influence or power in relation to another party in a conflict situation (Himes, 1980, p. 15).

By *technique* we mean an even more detailed "fine-tuning" mechanism—a further specification of tactics (Karrass, 1979, p. 183).

An example of the strategy-tactic-technique triumvirate is as follows: The strategic goal for a group of workers in a human service organization is to secure increased participation in the agency's policymaking body by means of an educational and political campaign. The tactics include persuasion and manipulation, supported by the "latent" combative threat of a strike. A technique, which might be used early in the process, is to have a "coffee hour" to which board members would be invited for the purpose of an informal chat about the matter.

Although the distinctions among strategy, tactics, and techniques are useful, particularly insofar as they remind us of the importance of viewing a conflict in terms of all these aspects, they should not become a preoccupying concern. Our treatment of modes of conflict management in subsequent chapters will take a rather relaxed posture toward the distinctions.

SUMMARY

In this chapter we presented a framework—composed of categories of interaction and modes of conflict management—for the analysis and management of conflict. We also noted related dimensions of conflict management, including the importance of rules and some basic guides to constructive personal relationships in conflict situations. The chapter concluded with definitions of *strategy, tactics,* and *techniques.*

NOTE

1. For a discussion of a number of these points regarding rules, see Deutsch (1977, pp. 379-380) and Himes (1980, pp. 223-228).

PART II

MANAGING CONFLICT

Chapter 4

OVERVIEW AND THE MODES
OF FORESTALLING, SIDESTEPPING,
AND GENERATING CONFLICT

OVERVIEW

A structural framework of conflict management was outlined in the preceding chapter. Now we turn to the process. This is depicted in the accompanying flow chart (Chart 4.1). The lettered references below refer to the boxes in this chart. Box F is the core of the conflict management process.

The starting point in the process is a perceived conflict (Box A). Perception in itself, however, is insufficient for making considered action decisions. *Confirmation* that a genuine conflict exists and an understanding of the factors that lead to and characterize the conflict require assessment (Box B). Assessment may lead to a decision either to act on the conflict or not to go any further in the process (Box C). If assessment results in the decision to go ahead with conflict managing activities, then the process continues (Box D).

Assessment is a complex activity. First, there needs to be clarity about one's own goals and certainty that the other party's objectives are actually (and significantly) opposed to them. Unnecessary conflict, due to misunderstanding, a lack of accurate information, or bad timing, is at best a waste—and may sometimes lead to disaster. Second, there needs to be an accurate diagnosis of the type of conflict. Third, there should be reasonable grounds for the judgment that the prospective conflict managing activity will be an appropriate and effective way of achieving the desired objectives. This involves a careful weighing of the broad range of likely benefits and costs in as complete a manner as is feasible. Fourth, there needs to be a comprehensive identification of the resources that would be available in the conflict situation. This process requires a realistic appraisal of your resources and those of your opponent: By *realistic* we mean those that could actually be mobilized and implemented in the type of conflict that is envisioned. Also, the determination (will), expertise, and availability for critical assignments of those who will be carrying the conflict, and their rear guard supporters, should be cautiously appraised, remembering how quickly enthusiasms may burn out in the face of mounting costs. Finally, the selection of the appropriate strategies, tactics, and techniques should be carefully evaluated, keeping in mind that a balance is desirable between forward planning and flexibility.

In some conflict situations, particularly those of a one-on-one character, there may not be time to plan ahead and carefully assess the situation. In the case of such "spontaneous" conflicts, one should try to pause for a moment and decide what's happening and why. At that point many of the previously cited mental steps can be quickly reviewed in terms of whether the wisest course of action is to plow ahead, sidestep, suspend the conflict, or otherwise try to extricate oneself from the situation.

The ability to make quick decisions "on one's feet" is an asset in conflict management. This rapid decision-making process is complicated by the strong emotional coloring that often accompanies it. Hence particular caution must be exercised to ensure that one doesn't become an *inadvertent* conflict participant, or, if a conflict does suddenly break out, that one is able to call a halt before it is too late.

Assuming that the decision to proceed with the conflict management process has been made, then it is important to identify the type of interaction that will characterize the encounter, for instance, one-on-one, representational, or third party (see Chart 3.1 in the preceding chapter and Box E in the flow chart). Once there is clarity on this matter, one should select the appropriate mode (modes) of conflict management (Box F). This involves an ongoing choice (and review/revision) of strategies, tactics, and techniques (Box G). Finally, there are the likely outcomes (there may be multiple results—and at different points in time) (Box H).

Although the process is depicted in Chart 4.1 as a one-way flow of events, the process may not be quite as clean and uncluttered in actual practice. There may well be a back-and-forth process among the stages as developments dictate reconsideration of prior operational decisions.

We will now turn to a key part of the process, the determination of the

CHART 4.1
Conflict Management: A Flow Chart

A	B	C
Existence of a Perceived Conflict	Assessment of Factors Prior to Action Decisions - affirmation of the existence of a genuine conflict - diagnosis as to type and sources of conflict - clarification as to goals of prospective action - identification of resources available to both parties - evaluation of costs/ benefits of likely outcomes	Decision to Terminate Process after Negative Assessment of Factors

OR

D

Decision to Engage in Conflict Managing Activities after Positive Assessment of Factors

F	E
Determination of Mode(s) of Conflict Management to be Employed: - forestalling/sidestepping - generating conflict - use of covert means - emergent agreement - direct negotiations - indirect or procedural means - exercise of authority/power	Identification of Category of Conflict Management Interaction - one-on-one - representational - third party - clinical

G	H
Selection of Strategies Tactics and Techniques	Outcomes: - immediate - medium term - long term

mode of conflict management and the selection of strategies and tactics (Boxes F and G). This area of concern will serve as the focus for the remainder of the book.

SECTION I: FORESTALLING
AND SIDESTEPPING CONFLICT

Let's now address ourselves to the first of the modes of conflict management, that is forestalling and sidestepping conflict.

In many situations the most effective way of managing an impending clash is to keep the conflict from developing, or to do a neat two-step around it. Although we hold strongly to the conviction that conflict may be necessary and justifiable under given circumstances, we readily acknowledge that in other situations it might well be unnecessary, unwise, and extremely destructive. And the prevention or avoidance of undesired conflicts is very much a part of effective conflict management. Our concern then, at this point, is with the strategies and tactics associated with averting unnecessary or too costly conflicts of interest and commitment.

PREVENTION

Prevention is the strategy of preference when there is a genuine potential in a situation or structure for the emergence of an *undesirable* conflict of interests or commitments. By *undesirable* we mean that conflict, in the given circumstances, is not likely to be the most effective way of gaining ones objectives—or that it will be too costly or destructive in various respects.

The situations in which there are a heightened potential for conflicts of interest/commitment to develop are those characterized by competition and/or pronounced differences in beliefs or desires. As we have already pointed out, competition, although different from conflict, frequently results in conflict. And though disagreement is basic to conflict, not all differences (even sharp ones) result in conflict. We can all think of many ways in which our views (from reactions to a movie to beliefs about the nature of the universe) diverge from those of other people, without our engaging in conflict with them. However, divergent commitments are the fertile soil from which many a conflict arises.

On a personal note, we might observe that a majority of the work-related conflicts that we have experienced, or observed, were unnecessary, undesirable, or inappropriately intense—and sometimes these unwarranted conflicts were very costly to the participants. Hence prevention, designed to keep competition and divergent views from being converted into unnecessary conflict, is a very important aspect of conflict management.

With these general comments as a preface we are now ready to consider some of the key tactics that are suggested by the *strategy of prevention*.

Increased Organizational Responsiveness

Generally speaking, many organizations show a tendency toward inflexibility, resistance to change, and a defensive rigidity in the face of criticism. There are many reasons for this. Some organizational managers and other elites who reap benefits from the status quo are likely to "dig in their heels" when the winds of change begin to swirl around them, or when faced with critical questioning. In many organizations, the reward system is oriented toward providing security for those who follow rules and stick to procedures, rather than offering incentives for the innovator and risk-taker. Routinization of activities is frequently used as a protective shield against the stress that may be produced when habituated behavior is interfered with, or reflective thought is called for. Deviations from routine frequently require added expenditures of effort and energy. For some people this itself is to be avoided at all costs.

Finally, there is often a problem of "false consciousness of interests," a phenomenon that we previously discussed. What happens is that a passionate commitment to the status quo, or a rejection of complaints out of hand, may be perceived as protecting one's self-interest. Although this is sometimes the case, there may well be the reverse consequence, that is, the nonaccommodation to changing circumstances and requirements may, in the medium and long run, prove to be counterproductive to one's organizational self-interest. After all, history is replete with examples of the response to "demands for bread" being, figuratively or literally, to "let them eat cake"—with the consequence that those giving such replies may lose their heads. Clearly, the cavalier dismissal of such demands, with the resultant disaster for those in positions of authority, was not in their "true" self-interest.

In our experience, it is one of the most important grounds for the generating of unnecessary conflict. An example of such behavior in the human services is the response of some professionalized agencies to the formation of client self-help groups. Not infrequently such groups, at the time they were first exerting significant interests of their own, were categorically denied a legitimate role in the helping process by various professionals. Only recently have their contributions been selectively appraised, with understanding. This has often led to some very unproductive conflicts and weakened legitimate criticism of self-help groups.

Another all-too-common example is the reaction of some academics to reasonable student requests for participation in decision-making and in staff evaluation. They respond in an intransigent manner, thus ensuring the emergence of unproductive conflictual situations.

In order to reduce the likelihood of such "unnecessary" conflicts arising, it is important to recognize the importance of deliberately *building in* "organizational responsiveness" as a tactic in the strategy of conflict prevention. For example, in an academic setting one might create an appeals structure (which includes student members) for the purpose of dealing with student grievances, or establish the policy that students may have their essay examinations evaluated by a second reader if they so desire.

Enhanced responsiveness can also be built into human service organizations if those holding positions of authority establish policies and procedures that reward risk-taking and accountability. Unfortunately, the resistance to such "rational" behavior may be great. I know of a public agency in which it was taking up to six months to respond to a letter from outside the organization. This was due to refusal by the person in charge of the relevant department to allow reasonable decentralization of decision making and accountability—even in respect to signing letters.

The development of appropriate organizational norms, rules, and procedures can also enhance responsiveness. Agency leadership can promote the idea that effectiveness in service provision and in ensuring justice for users-of-services will take priority over in-group (staff) solidarity. This can be reinforced by a "open-door" system that allows complaints to move "upstairs" quickly once there has been an opportunity for the relevant staff to cope with them at lower levels.

Even physical arrangements (discussed in an earlier chapter) can encourage or inhibit responsiveness. Providing persons who have complaints, or hold "deviant ideas," with a comfortable and "egalitarian" physical arrangement can be of assistance. So too would such informal behaviors as showing respect by not keeping people waiting. It might well be useful to encourage the idea that the user-of-service be perceived as either a desired consumer, or a "guest," or a combination of both.

Frequently, the procedures adopted to enhance organizational responsiveness will be relatively formalized and rule-regulated (e.g., participation in a joint worker-client body). However, there is also much opportunity in less formal and one-on-one interactions to convey and reinforce the organization's commitment to responsiveness.

Early Identification of Latent Conflicts

In several workshops I conducted, participants raised the question of how to cope with antagonism between two workers from the same unit, both of whom applied for promotion to a given position, with one succeeding and the other failing. One of the interesting aspects of this query was the questioners' emphasis on what should be done "after the fact." In other words, little attention was given to what might have been done ahead of time to lessen or prevent the conflict between the workers.

Because there is an inherent potential for conflict in this situation, it is important to prevent the competitiveness from becoming conflictual. An aware supervisor or administrator, for instance, could discuss the implications of the competition, and the prevailing ground rules, with the staff prior to the decision on the promotion. Once the selection is made, further individual meetings with the unsuccessful and successful candidates might be held. In the discussion with the "loser," the reasons for the decision might be elaborated, the strengths of the worker in his or her present position should be emphasized (if it can be done honestly), and future possibilities might be explored. By indicating that the decision wasn't made by the competitor, any negative feelings that are ventilated could be directed toward the decision-maker, rather than the colleague.

The legitimacy of disappointment, and even anger, needs to be recognized. In the meeting with the successful candidate the positive contributions of the "loser" in that person's present position should be highlighted, as well as the appropriateness of that individual having competed for the position. Also, suggestions might be offered on how the successful candidate could interact in an effective and supportive manner with the unsuccessful one.

This is an example of the early identification of latent conflict, with subsequent action designed to lessen the likelihood of competition becoming conflictual. In this situation the supervisor/administrator is involved in representational interaction. However, the relationship between the two workers is primarily of a one-on-one character.

"Hot Lines"

The term *hot line* has been popularized by the claimed existence of a special telephone hook-up between the leaders of the United States and the USSR. The purpose of this device is to reduce the likelihood of an "accidental" conflict, particularly one involving nuclear weapons.

This same tactic is useful in more ordinary circumstances. For instance, if some differences exist between two members of an organization, and written memos appear to have the potentiality for escalating those differences into a conflict, then a telephone call, a luncheon meeting, or just a face-to-face conference might prevent this from happening. Such procedures might have been agreed upon ahead of time as a desirable tactic in the case of potential conflicts.

By hot lines, then, we mean the use of direct communication devices designed to reduce the likelihood of differences or misunderstandings unnecessarily "exploding" into conflicts.

"Institutionalized Dissenters"

A person may not be willing to express views counter to those of others in a situation because of the fear of alienating them, or of being vulnerable to a retaliatory response. This is especially true when there is an unequal relationship among the participants—for example, if one is interacting with one's boss or a high-status person. The consequent failure to articulate divergent views may result in differences being submerged until they emerge at a later time, more sharply, in the form of conflict. In policymaking groups, such reluctance to disagree often results in poorer policy outcomes because not all of the relevant objections are considered before the decisions are made.

One somewhat stylized way in which to deal with this problem of "inhibited disagreement" is to give a participant in the discussion the brief to be a "dissenter." In a one-to-one situation this can take the form of specifically inviting the other party to articulate all the objections they can think of in respect to a given position or policy. In a larger, ongoing group, the role of dissenter may be formalized and rotated. For instance, one week one person may be assigned to be the "devil's advocate," while the next week another person may be asked to take the dissenter's role. Such a procedure could become an established part of such meetings.

The advantage of such an institutionalized dissenter role is that it permits disagreement to be expressed without exposing the dissenter to the potential costs of incurring the wrath or disaffection of other participants. The value of this tactic in preventing conflict is that it may allow, at low or reduced cost, persons to disagree before their differences harden into conflictual positions. Also, it lessens the likelihood of recriminations, which may lead to conflict, resulting from some participants claiming that others in the situation should have spoken up if they didn't agree before the decision was arrived at. This type of recrimination is likely to occur if the decision proved to have an undesirable outcome.

One caution! If your supervisor tries out an idea on you, your reactions should be controlled by accepted conventions and discretion. In other words, if you think the idea or proposal being advanced, and to which you are asked to "candidly" react, is unworkable or undesirable, you are probably well advised to express such views in a tactful and controlled fashion, rather than being "brutally frank" or offensive.

Exposure of Differences Prior to Becoming Conflicts

Any teacher will have encountered situations in which students don't know whether or not they disagree with something the teacher has said but are reluctant to raise questions. This may be due to personal timidity, or to disillusioning life experiences in which questioning has resulted in ridicule or retaliation. The skillful teacher will use various techniques to bring out differences: These include providing a reassuring, "accepting" milieu; conveying a sense that no genuine question is inappropriate or a waste of time; and spelling out controversial implications of a statement or position, thus legitimatizing disagreement.

In many organizational or personal situations a slight hesitation in concurring on the part of another person, or a puzzled look, may suggest the desirability of looking further for possibly divergent views, even if half-formed. Or one may double-check decisions already agreed to in order to ensure that they were not unintentionally coerced, or too quickly arrived at.

Although this tactic of trying to "expose differences" is somewhat similar to several of the preceding ones (e.g., the institutionalized dissenter), it often varies in its application, particularly in terms of the nature and subtlety of the techniques associated with it. The "ground rules" for employing this tactic are less clear, and the norms governing the usage less explicit, than in the case of some of the other tactics.

This tactic may be appropriate in representational or one-on-one interactions and in formal or informal settings. Its utility is to bring out possible hidden differences. And this type of early identification of submerged or even only faintly recognized differences may prevent conflict from developing belatedly.

Diffusion of Conflict Managing Skills

This tactic consists of transmitting and diffusing conflict managing strategies, tactics, and associated techniques through an organization by formal and informal discussion, staff development programs, or similar means. It may also be employed in third-party interventions with clients or disputants in a conflict. For instance, instruction in preventive tactics might well be included in subjects on parenting, or communication in marriage.

A question that may arise at this point is, does it put me or my group at a disadvantage if I share my knowledge of conflict management with others, particularly with potential adversaries? This issue was raised with me by a group of executives at a seminar on conflict management. They were concerned that similar sessions for workers in their organizations might have an adverse effect on their effectiveness as executives in managing conflict with their employees.

Fortunately, this is a concern that can be dealt with in a straightforward and reassuring manner. In our experience, effective conflict management does not usually depend on a "secret" bag of tricks designed to surprise an unsuspecting opponent. It is, in fact, usually more advantageous to engage in conflictual or potentially conflictual interactions with people who are knowledgeable about the strategies and tactics of conflict management than with those who are "innocent." The lack of relevant knowledge and skills, plus not knowing the rules, is a major impediment to effective conflict management. To be an effective participant in a conflict situation requires an understanding of the requisite roles and how they are to be performed. So the more widely the strategies and tactics of conflict management are known, the better it will be for all of us.

Let us now look at a conflict (hypothetical, of course) that is, in its own way, every bit as dramatic as the medical soap operas that appear daily on the TV screen. In our commentary on the events we shall be concerned with what might have been; that is, how the conflict might have been contained, reduced in intensity/scope, or prevented.

The public became aware of the conflict through media headlines such as the following:

— 25,000 People on Waiting List for Admission to Hospitals For "Elective" Surgery
— Hospital Beds Closed Because of Nurse Shortage
— Patient Dies After Being Refused Admission to Hospital Because no Beds Available
— Nurses Take Industrial Action: Hospitals in Crisis
— Hospital Management and Nurses Accuse Each Other of Bad Faith
— Issues in Hospital Dispute To Go To Arbitration
— Non-Nursing Hospital Staff Go On Strike
— Nurses' Concerns Understandable Say Doctors But Deplore Their Tactics
— Nurses Claim Government Went Back On Its Promises
— Head of Governmental Department Claims Additional Resources Have Been Given To Hospitals! Charges Nurses With Being Irresponsible and Unreasonable

These were the overt outcroppings of the conflict. But what was the story behind the headlines?

BACKGROUND FACTORS

The roots of this conflict go deep. They include such entrenched attitudes and social arrangements as male attitudes toward women and the domination of nursing by the medical profession; the view that members of the helping professions (i.e., nurses) would betray their "caring" responsibilities if they were so "self-interested" as to take industrial action; and the apprenticeship system of training nurses within hospitals.

Precipitating conditions included the following:

— increased consumer pressure on municipal hospitals, partly because improved health insurance benefits for those using such facilities raised consumer expectations in regard to health care
— shortage of financial resources available to the municipality and hospitals
— increased stress on nurses due to the introduction of high-tech equipment and the changing functions of hospitals, resulting in more emphasis on "acute care"
— increased employment opportunities for women in a variety of fields
— transition in the training of nurses from hospitals to institutions of higher education
— changes in the roles of women and an increased assertiveness on their part
— "demystification" and questioning of high status professions (e.g., medicine) and many institutional practices
— increased militancy in other "white-collar" occupations as well as the demonstration of muscle by nonnursing hospital workers
— enhanced expectations as to working conditions (including relief from rotating shift work)
— decreased legitimacy of authoritarian management practices
— elimination of no-strike clause from the constitution of the Nursing Federation
— competition with the Nurses' Federation from other unions seeking to represent nurses
— more "militant" leadership within the Nursing Federation

PREVENTIVE TACTICS: USE AND MISUSE

This hypothetical example has enough similarities to some real-life conflicts that we can easily identify, without unduly stretching the bounds of plausibility, what might have occurred in respect to the use and misuse of preventive tactics.

To begin with, some hospitals have demonstrated inadequate institutional responsiveness to changes in authority structures and gender relationships. We will hypothesize (in our example) that the attitudes within the nursing hierarchy and in the overall decision-making apparatus was quite authoritarian and traditional. Hence the procedures in the hospitals were not conducive to genuine participation by the nurses (particularly at "lower levels"). In turn, this meant there was inadequate provision for the early identification of latent conflicts and exposure of difference in a nonadversarial atmosphere.

The nurses believed that their complaints were not being taken seriously and that on many critical issues they simply weren't being listened to. The objective evidence provided strong support for this perception. For instance, several studies alerting management and the government to latent problems and making recommendations for change had been filed without serious consideration or action. Furthermore, at meetings of nurses the director of the Department of Integrated Human Services and Resources (the funding agency) had told the nurses that there was no way to meet their demand for an addition in the number of budgeted nurse positions to meet the increased stress and consumer demand. In fact, they were told they should look for work elsewhere if they couldn't accept the situation as it was.

The situation was aggravated by an across-the-board cut in funding for the hospitals. This directive, which came from "on high" and without grass roots discussion, seriously aggravated the situation.

The nurses, angry and frustrated, were hampered in taking effective action by their own inexperience, lack of support from some top nursing administrators, and an uncertainty as to whether industrial action by nurses was justifiable. Part of the reason for the nonresponsiveness and authoritarianism of the officials and management was their assumption that the historical passivity of nurses on such issues would continue. Furthermore, they correctly judged that nurses suffered from a lack of training and experience in conflict managing skills.

One of the arenas in which the inexperience of the nurses became most evident was in public relations. Although they had a strong case to put before the public, this was not well exploited.

Ultimately, as the nurses became increasingly militant, many of their demands were met—but only after they took serious industrial action with inevitably unpleasant consequences for consumers and working relationships. The "lesson" for the nurses was that coercion is the only method that seems to work—even claimed nonexistent financial resources suddenly became available under pressure.

Most of the disruptions and other costs associated with the conflict (and likely to be part of future clashes in the hospitals) could have been reduced or lessened if:

(1) There had been more organizational responsiveness, thus allowing for adequate and timely changes in authority structures, interprofessional relationships, gender attitudes, and educational programs.
(2) The nurses had been encouraged, in a nonadversarial atmosphere, to voice their concerns and to perceive that they were really being listened to.

(3) There had been adequate communication devices among the different participants before the conflict got out of hand.

(4) The decision-making systems within the hospitals had sufficient representation of diverse interests and perspectives (and made use of institutionalized dissenters) so that earlier and more effective responses to the emerging crisis would have been forthcoming.

(5) All parties had been more skillful in conflict management.

Pause for Reflection

Several situations drawn from "real life" are described below. Identify the "errors" that were made that turned these latent disputes into overt conflicts. How would you have handled these situations?

Situation 1: A private (voluntary) human service organization found itself, unexpectedly, in a financial crisis. It was decided by management that 25% of the professional staff would have to be retrenched. The staff, as a staff, was not brought into the picture officially, although some information was leaked. Requests by staff members for clarification of the situation were refused by management. Suddenly, one day, all of the professional staff that were to be dismissed were visited by managerial staff and asked to clear their desks by the end of that working day. The dismissed workers were offered severance pay. The end result was a dispute that was never fully resolved and continued to hurt the agency's standing and functioning for several years.

Situation 2: The ward attendants in a psychiatric hospital indirectly let it be known that they would like to have more input in the decision-making process concerning policies and ward procedures. Subsequently, they were invited into staff meetings, at which they sat at the end of a long table and were called upon for opinions infrequently, and usually after higher-status participants had spoken. The ward attendants were addressed by their first names while the M.D.s were addressed by title and last name. After a few months the attendants seldom bothered to show up for the staff meetings. Subsequently, overt dissatisfaction about their role in the hospital was expressed by the ward attendants. Conflict over participation in decision making then broke out, involving not only the attendants, but the nurses as well.

Situation 3: Two students, representing an entire class, met with the instructor and raised questions about the value of the content being taught. They suggested that either the subject matter be reconsidered or the course be made elective, rather than compulsory. The teacher politely dismissed the concerns of the students. When an academic administrator was told about the situation by a student, and broached the matter to the instructor, he was told that it was a "tempest in a teapot" stirred up by a few malcontents in the class. The instructor continued to ignore the developing discontent and took no action. Eventually, a heated dispute broke out over the matter—and the student association and faculty engaged in conflict. In addition, the instructor resigned in anger, being critical of both the students and the administrator, claiming that the latter should have supported him without reservation.

Situation 4: The workers in a commercial organization reported to one of the junior executives that their counterparts in similar companies were provided with an additional day of vacation. This "report" was given informally, and by way of being relevant information, rather than constituting an official request or demand for equivalent benefits. The junior executive suggested to their boss that the possibility of an additional holiday be discussed with the staff. In response, the senior executive turned down the suggestion, saying to the junior worker: "Don't you realize it's a continuing battle between them (the workers) and us (management)—and you shouldn't give them anything you don't have to." Although no overt conflict emerged, a number of the workers became alienated and the quantity and quality of their work deteriorated.

Situation 5: There were rumors in an agency that women members of the staff were finding it more difficult than men to be promoted to supervisory/administrative positions. No action was taken by anyone in response to these rumors. Six months later a charge of gender discrimination was filed against the agency.

We have been concerned, thus far, with the strategy of prevention, that is, "forestalling" conflicts from developing or intensifying. However, there are occasions when a conflict has arisen but one of the participants does not want to participate. After all, as the saying goes, it takes "two to tango."

What do you do if you don't want to become involved in a conflictual interaction? Well, you may try to "sidestep" the situation. In other words, you engage in some form of *avoidance* strategy.

AVOIDANCE

There are many good reasons for wishing to avoid a given conflict: The potential costs may appear to be too great; the accessible resources could be clearly inadequate, thus making a successful outcome most unlikely; there might be a genuine danger of uncontrollable escalation; the situation and timing might be undesirable; or there may be a better way of accomplishing one's goals. Of course, another important justification for not engaging in conflict would be that one's objectives are not really appropriate or legitimate.

The other side of the coin is that people sometimes try to avoid a conflict, although it may be necessary, fully justified, and arises at an opportune time. This may be because it is thought that engaging in conflict is "not nice," or because it is too painful. Related to this may be a failure to recognize that conflicts of interest are a normal part of social life. Certainly, for many people the personal discomfort (a cost) they feel in the face of conflict is the controlling factor. Yet, the effort to avoid real conflict by "masking" it often proves to be an illusionary solution with unforeseen costs. As a mediator pointed out during a family conflict situation in China: "You can't wrap fire in paper."

There are many ways to avoid conflict. Four readily recognizable tactics are denial, flight, relinquishment, and suspension.

Denial

The avoidance of a conflict, despite the presence of genuine conflictual elements in the situation, may be accomplished by the psychological process of denial, that is, by refusing to acknowledge that the circumstances are as they appear to be to others. The use of denial may result from anxiety, from the lack of a "correct" understanding ("false consciousness") of the situation, or because relevant information is not available. Whatever the reasons, though, denial represents a means by which one may attempt to avoid conflict.

Illustrative of the denial tactic at work is the refusal by a "peace at any price" chairperson to acknowledge that participants in a meeting are in conflict. This is sometimes expressed, in a comment by the chair, to the effect that "it was so nice to have had a lively discussion. Although some minor differences exist, as is to be expected in any group, I'm certain that we all believe, basically, in the same things." Such a summary may follow what was obviously a most fundamental conflict over goals or interests.

In my experience this is not an atypical tactic of conflict management in situations involving close personal relationships, or in organizations that put a premium on harmony, consensus, and "politeness."

Flight

It is hard to fight when there is no one with which to fight. Hence one decisive way in which to avoid a conflict is to get out of the situation by physically removing oneself. Structural changes in an organization can accomplish the same purpose; for example, a person's work assignment and interactional patterns might be altered, or there may be a change in role definitions. Certainly, flight, in the broad sense of the word, is one avoidance tactic to be considered.

Relinquishment

There are times when the better part of valor is to withdraw so as to be able to survive to fight again another day. One may avoid a continuing conflict by disengaging from a situation at the most minimal cost possible. There are a variety of face-saving techniques that might be employed in such a situation (e.g., contending that the explicit objectives had been intentionally inflated as a bargaining device and that the realistic expectations have been achieved, hence there is no need to continue the struggle). Relinquishment, then, is one option in avoiding conflict, or further conflict.

Suspension

It is desirable on certain occasions to disengage, temporarily, from a conflict situation. This might be by means of a "truce," or a less formal technique. Of course, a suspension may even be disguised as relinquishment for purposes of deceiving one's adversary. Suspension may be useful in a variety of ways: It can allow for a "regrouping" of resources or adding to the existing resource pool; or it might provide for the conflict to be resumed at a more advantageous time or site.

With the discussion of the above tactics we come to the end of the discussion of forestalling and sidestepping conflict!

The next section of this chapter stands in striking contrast to the one just concluded. It is concerned with generating conflict.

SECTION II: GENERATING CONFLICT

It may seem strange to include the "generating of conflict" within this volume. After all, isn't conflict management all about resolving or eliminating conflict? The answer is a resounding no! As was pointed out earlier, the term *conflict management* (rather than *conflict resolution*) is employed because it is inclusive. Conflict management avoids the limiting assumption that the goal of all effective conflict related activity should be its resolution. Our viewpoint on this terminology is related to the point made earlier that conflict can be a constructive, indeed vital, aspect of the human drama.

When, then, should one intentionally set about to create conflict? The "generating of conflict" is an appropriate mode of conflict management when nonconflictual means are ineffectual in promoting or attaining positive professional and social goals; when the power/influence resources to conduct conflict effectively are available; and when it is estimated that the costs of *not* engaging in conflict would be unacceptably high.

With this clarification of the rationale for the inclusion of the "conflict generating" mode we now turn to the first of the relevant *strategies*.

EXPLICATING LATENT CONFLICT AND IDENTIFYING AREAS IN WHICH CONFLICTUAL ACTION WOULD BE DESIRABLE

Due to socialization or deliberate indoctrination, people sometimes fail to recognize that they are being treated unfairly or taken advantage of, or that their legitimate interests are being suppressed. Equally important, even when there is recognition that the situation is unjust or intolerable the victims may not believe that they can or should engage in conflict in order to change the status quo.

One of the tactics that addresses this lack of awareness, or defeatism, about the possibilities of overcoming the situation is "consciousness-raising."

Consciousness-Raising

The term *consciousness-raising* usually refers to a type of group "self-help" activity in which people who share a common concern, experience, or characteristic (e.g., gender), meet together. In these sessions the participants seek a heightened and, presumably, more accurate awareness of their common place in the scheme of things and of their shared problems or concerns, and the underlying reasons for them. In addition, there is usually an exploration of the possibilities for corrective action.

Since many of the participants, at the onset of such meetings, may have had an "imperfect" understanding and "false consciousness" about their circumstances and interests, the purpose of the "consciousness-raising" activities is to create a "truer" picture of reality.

From the perspective of conflict management it is a tactic aimed at explicating latent conflicts of interests and commitment and identifying areas in which conflictual actions would be desirable. This tactic, in its general sense, has been useful not only in the civil rights and feminist movements but also in giving certain occupational groups a more realistic perspective. For instance, nurses have for some time recognized that their interests may well differ in many situations from doctors' and hospital managers': The elimination of "no strike" clauses by nursing associations in various states and countries is an example of this. Even formerly passive consumers have had their "consciousness raised" by people such as Ralph Nader and organizations like the Consumers' Union. And sexually harassed persons, or victims of malpractice, are now much more likely to engage in conflictual action in order to protect themselves or to get compensation for wrongs done to them.

Exposing a False Consensus

In certain situations one's beliefs or interests may be put in jeopardy by the desire of some of the persons involved to press for "consensual agreements," even if the consensus is questionable or coerced. Informal social controls are frequently used to avoid rupturing such "pressured agreements," including subtle devices, sometimes unintentional, like audible sighs among participants when an apparent consensus is challenged. Many people, in order to avoid conflict, go along with such maneuvers. In some situations "falseness" of the consensus is not even recognized.

Hence a potent tactic in generating desirable conflict is to explicate areas in dispute, thus challenging and exposing "pseudo" or "pressured" consensual outcomes.

Providing Opportunities for the Articulation of Significant Differences

Differences by themselves do not automatically lead to conflicts. But the explication and articulation of significant differences, particularly those of interest or commitment, may lead to, and even be a condition of, the emergence of conflict. This suggests that providing the opportunity for an awareness and expression of such differences may be an important tactic in generating conflict. Insisting on the full discussion of issues, and supporting the right of persons to espouse minority or unpopular views, may also contribute to prosocial conflictual behavior. For instance, in view of the "conforming tendencies" of many groups, a deliberate technique, such as the chairperson of a meeting praising those who present deviant views, could prove to be very useful.

It is not enough to recognize the positive aspects of engaging in conflict; there must also be the wherewithal to cope successfully with a conflict situation. This leads to the next strategy in generating conflict—that of providing the resources for the successful conduct of conflict, and creating confidence that such action can lead to productive outcomes.

CREATING CONFLICT MANAGING CAPABILITIES

One of the most important tactics in implementing the strategy of creating conflict managing capabilities is identifying power/influence resources.

Identifying Power/Influence Resources

In a previous chapter we noted the wide range of power/influence resources that can play a part in managing conflict. The listing included some resources that are frequently overlooked, or not usually perceived as resources.

One of the most useful tactics in creating conflict managing capabilities is carefully to identify and evaluate available power/influence resources. For instance, the workers in an agency may not realize how much capacity they have for forcing a superordinate (e.g., administrator) to expend "unproductive" time and energy in coping with their repeated complaints. And the identification of this power resource might encourage them to enter the fray with a reasonable chance of success.

Generating Resources

Identification of resources is an important tactic but it may still be that the resources at hand are insufficient for the successful conduct of conflict. Hence, another tactic is to strengthen the resource base: This may be in any of the areas of power resource suitable for the struggle that is to be initiated. For instance, the provision of expertise, or the creating of an alliance, might be very useful ways of helping to generate additional resources, thus improving the opportunities for successful conflict management.

In addition to knowing what resources are available and strengthening the weak areas, it is often important to build the confidence of potential conflict participants before they are willing to make the decision to take conflictual types of action. The next tactic is concerned with this requirement.

Developing Confidence in Conflict Management

It is important not only to possess the resources and knowledge that are prerequisites for successful conflict management, but one must also have the confidence to use them in actual conflict engagements. This tactic, that of building such confidence, is frequently overlooked in the training of human service workers. We believe that the provision of conflict experience through simulations and coaching are important techniques of building the requisite confidence, for instance, role-playing experiences in conflict management classes and workshops. Also, the introduction of an "interrogator role" when student briefs are presented might be helpful. In addition, the greater use of oral examination in education for the human service occupations might be a good idea. All of these techniques are useful in building confidence in one's ability to cope effectively in conflict management situations.

On the basis of the prior discussion of principles and tactics keep in mind the following action applications:

Action Guide!

(1) Caution: An apparent disinclination by you to engage in conflict gives your opponent an advantage. The demonstration of a fear of conflict is rarely an effective way of preventing it.

(2) Don't permit an excessive concern with social approval or politeness to keep you from exposing a false consensus or taking issue with a coerced agreement. Naturally, the generation of conflict should be done carefully and in as nonabrasive a manner as possible.

SUMMARY

The chapter opened with an overview of the conflict management process. This was followed by a discussion of the strategies and tactics of the forestalling/sidestepping and conflict generation modes of conflict management.

Chapter 5

COVERT MEANS

Even though a conflict exists, one or both of the combatants may deem it unwise to engage in overt methods of conflict management. In such circumstances the choice of weapons may range from passive resistance to concealment, or even to the active use of clandestine means. These various forms of silent or hidden means of managing conflict are clustered under the heading of "Covert Means."

This mode of conflict management is likely to come into play when there is considerable disparity in the power resources of the adversaries. The more powerful may use covert means in managing conflict in the hope of quietly containing or outsmarting the weaker opponent without the costs and potential uncertainties (e.g., escalation) of overt conflict. Covert means are seen in such situations as being expedient and likely to limit potential damage.

For the less powerful, though, the rationale for the use of covert means may be quite different. The weaker adversary is likely to use this mode of conflict management when the resources to engage in overt conflict are inadequate, or the likely costs of a direct confrontation are unacceptably high. There are also those conflict situations in which contenders are very unequal in terms of power resources and the weaker party is unable to get the stronger one to "come to the table." Adversaries with overwhelming power often see no need to engage in such rule-regulated conflict management activities as joint problem-solving, negotiation, and so forth. They may argue that if they can get what they want without engaging in overt conflict management, why do so?

Another reason people may use covert means is that they find it very difficult, psychologically, to get involved in direct conflict situations.

Finally, covert action may be what an actor is most skilled in, or believes will be most effective.

The inclusion of covert strategies, tactics, and techniques in this volume is primarily to assist readers in defending themselves against such means—in other words, to prevent victimization. A case can be made for the active use of covert activities when confronting crushing power employed to prevent the expression of legitimate interests by open means. Even in such instances it is preferable, *if feasible*, to try to create mechanisms that will permit desirable means of conflict management to be used.

The invocation of moral commitments, or the identification of unethical means being used with a warning of counteraction, may lessen or eliminate the need to employ covert means in self-defense. Or, in some instances, "dirty tricks" can be deflected without responding in like manner.

However, in some serious situations the use of covert means on behalf of prosocial objectives can be justified. These are situations in which all other reasonable courses of action are precluded and the potential damage (costs) of *not* using covert means is great.

The desire for success, though, is not in itself sufficient justification for the use of covert means—unless the other conditions we have stipulated also exist.

It is evident that the use of the clandestine means discussed in this chapter raises serious ethical questions and should be employed only after serious and careful soul-searching. One should make every effort to avoid easy rationalizations in such decision making.

Covert means are not highly structured in terms of rules, although some normative constraints usually do operate in human service agencies. For example, although a person might spread rumors in order to discredit an opponent, that same individual might well draw the line at planting a bomb. Note: Covert means may be used in either one-on-one or representational types of conflict transactions.

Now we turn to the first of the covert *strategies*.

PASSIVE RESISTANCE OR CONCEALMENT

When resources are quite limited, or potential costs too great, passive resistance or concealment may be substituted for more active and overt conflict strategies. Not surprisingly, relative powerlessness is likely to contribute to this strategic choice. The powerful are less likely to have to use this stratagem, although they may choose to employ it because of its apparent "efficiency" (i.e., low cost, positive outcomes). In addition, individual temperamental preferences may play a part in the choice of passive resistance or concealment. So, too, categories of people (e.g., women), because of their socialization and societal expectations, may become accustomed to using this approach. Again, such a pattern is likely to be linked to power considerations.

There are three *tactics* associated with the *strategy* of passive resistance or concealment: negativism, noncompliance, and "stonewalling."

Negativism

We have all encountered persons who, by appearance, body language, or terse verbalization, manifest disagreement, hurt, or aggressiveness, without overtly engaging in conflict. This tactic is often difficult for an adversary to confront directly, hence it may be effective. However, there is always the risk that a negativistic approach might generate retaliatory responses, some of which may be quite painful, such as isolating (physically or socially), ignoring, circumventing, or even dismissing. Too often, at the individual level, the tactic of negativism is adopted almost out of habit, rather than representing a conscious selection as the most effective means for accomplishing one's objectives.

Noncompliance

This tactic runs the gamut from simple noncooperation to the conscious, though covert, sabotaging of policies by inadequate implementation. In some organizations and situations it is probably quite widespread.

Noncompliance, which may be employed at the individual or conflict group level, should be distinguished from "overt noncooperation," which is an active tactic. The use of noncompliance raises important ethical issues. It requires careful consideration of the possible advantage of overt action as an alternative.

Stonewalling

In the case of stonewalling, the line between tactic and technique is murky. However, there are some instances in which it has been adopted as a tactic. By stonewalling we mean the adamant refusal to comment about something, or to admit to an action or statement. It may sometimes prove effective, but it can have disastrous consequences when one doesn't get away with it.

MANIPULATION

Manipulation has, in common with the prior strategy, a covert character, although it is more active and less defensive. In the political arena this strategy often goes by the term "Machiavellianism," named, of course, after the famous statesman. One definition of Machiavellianism is "the willingness and ability to use guile, deceit, and other opportunistic strategies in interpersonal relations in order to manipulate other people" (Geis, cited in Rubin & Brown, 1975, p. 189; also see Geis & Christie, 1970). It can apply to one-on-one, representational, or even third-party conflict management interactions.

An important element in most definitions of manipulation is the creation of a false impression by surreptitious means, either by action or by inaction. For some, manipulation is perceived as a strategic alternative to authoritarian or power-coercive models. Among the key ideas that characterize most manipulation models are hiding one's true motives; the covert exploitation of the dependency of one party on the other (Leavitt, 1972, chap. 15); and masking the fact that one's actions are, in fact, designed to influence or "coerce" the recipient of the manipulative actions.

Examples of manipulative techniques that human service workers should be aware of include (1) the good guy-bad guy setup, and (2) the use of physical arrangements at meetings and conferences to "load the dice." The first of these is the highly publicized (on TV) device of having two interrogators, one taking a hard line and the other a soft approach. They work together on the recipient of their not-so-tender attentions until that individual develops a dependency on the good guy, thus eventually complying with that interrogator's advice.

A second technique (really a cluster of several techniques) is the organization of the physical arrangement of a meeting room so that it disadvantages one of the parties in a conflict situation. For example, the participant who has to face a nonshaded window is at a distinct disadvantage in terms of "reading" other people's expressions, as well as suffering from general distraction. Other related techniques are the arrangement of the seating in such a way as to divide one's opponents from a support group; the creation of a height differential situation so that the subordinate-superordinate relationship is reinforced; the provision of a "security blanket" (e.g., table) for one side while leaving the other comparatively denuded of this type of "protection"; and to make access to required facilities more difficult for one side than the other.

Our discussion of such techniques is not intended to encourage their use, but rather to ensure that human service workers will be able to defend themselves against such actions. This raises the broader question of the ethics of manipulative strategies, tactics, and techniques. It may reasonably be contended the human service workers should not, normally, initiate such strategies and tactics. There are also practical grounds for challenging the appropriateness and desirability of employing these measures. For instance, fundamental harm may be done to relationships and future attempts at conflict management if the manipulative efforts are exposed.

Despite the above concerns, however, the use of an "active" covert strategy, such as manipulation, may be justified in certain circumstances. Brager and Holloway (1978, pp. 26-27) argue that in given situations "it is not only acceptable but appropriate for a worker to 'go underground' in his efforts to effect positive change." They do caution that human service workers using "unobtrusive means" should adhere to explicit guidelines in order to "steer the practitioner in an ethical direction."

It should be said that some degree of manipulation often creeps into the use of a number of other strategies and tactics as well. However, the distinction between a stratagem for which manipulation is the core and an approach in which it is peripheral is really a matter of kind, not just of degree.

With these preliminary comments about manipulation as a backdrop, we will now turn to a specifying of selected manipulative *tactics*.

Deceit

This tactic covers the ground from mild distortion to outright dishonesty and lying. In conflict situations, deceit involves misrepresentation, providing misleading or false information, withholding material, or otherwise creating distortions in the communications network. The initiation and dissemination of rumors and other false reports are techniques that fall within this same tactical category. Although there is a slogan in sports to the effect that "nice guys finish last" in many types of conflictual situations, particularly those that involve more than one episode, the use of deceit may be counterproductive. This is so because the user of such tactics/techniques, if "found out," may be irretrievably discredited. The ethical problems associated with this tactic are apparent.

Disadvantaging

The technique mentioned in the introductory section of this chapter, that is, the "unfair" arrangement of the meeting room so as to put one of the parties in a weaker, more vulnerable, or less effective position, is part of a disadvantaging *tactic*. It involves the unfair "stacking of the cards" against one of the participants in a conflict; here again, the ethical dilemmas are evident.

Seduction

This tactic refers to the use of questionable enticements, including the "purchase" of support, in order to influence the outcome in a conflict. What makes the enticements manipulative is that the motives and/or intended outcomes are hidden, or at least not revealed. One technique of this type is *conscience stretching*. It is interestingly described in an authoritative textbook on the craft of espionage, under the heading, "Broadening the Arena of Conscience."

> The point is this: the principal must not only get the prospective agent into the habit of accepting his largesse; he must enable him to rationalize it so that it will not be a constant burden on his conscience—After Emily had done a string of small favours, her conscience had learned to justify them—or, in the jargon of espionage specialists, her "arena of conscience had been expanded." In taking the prospective agent up to the point of actual recruitment, the principal never asks him to do anything that lies beyond this arena. (Copeland, 1978, p. 128)

There is also the admonition, in the same volume, that only attractions that have "Novocaine suspicion deadeners" built into them should be offered (p. 126). In other words, ones' real motives should be well disguised.

A second technique within this tactic is that conveyed by the usual sexual meaning of seduction. This device was referred to by a woman politician in a chat with the author as "bedroom conversion." Its potential for serving as a means of influence, under certain circumstances, probably requires no elaboration. It becomes even more coercive if "blackmail" is introduced into the situation subsequent to the seduction. Although seduction in its literal sense is probably not a frequent instrument of conflict management in human service agencies, it does occur. However, seduction, in its broader meaning, as discussed below, is not uncommon.

A third technique is the "buying" of influence through pandering to the irresponsible or unjustified goals, interests, or desires of potential or actual adversaries. The use of pay increases, promotions, or other "perks" to "buy" support is an example of this. This can be differentiated from bribery because it may be "legal" and technically legitimate. But, depending on the motivation and means employed, it may well fit within the tactic of seduction.

A fourth technique, co-optation, may also fall into the category of seduction, although the term *co-optation* is sometimes broadened, inappropriately, to include perfectly desirable and legitimate modes of behavior. One definition of co-optation is the process of absorbing new members into supposed positions of leadership or policymaking in an organization to avert threats by those persons to the power of those dominating the organization.[1] Some "token" appointments to boards or committees fit this definition, as do some employee participation schemes. But not all offers of participation to members of less powerful groups are unprincipled co-optation. Such actions may, in fact, be designed genuinely to broaden participation in decision making, and sometimes even a "token" appointee may be the opening wedge. There is a danger that all measures involving the introduction of "representatives" from a weaker category, group, or class (or gender or ethnic group) might be dismissed as co-optation, rather than as progress toward a more equitable and effective decision-making system. Nevertheless, co-optation, in the meaning given to it here, does occur and can be a very manipulative and destructive technique. Interestingly enough, sometimes what starts out as co-optation ends up with a takeover by the newly introduced interest group. Gamson (1968, p. 137) depicts the uncertainty element in the process with the following comment:

> Both the partisan's and authority's fears about co-optation are valid fears. Co-optation invariably involves some mixture of outcome modification and social control and the exact mix is difficult to determine in advance. The authority who opposes co-opting the hostile element fears that outcome modification will dominate the mix; the partisan who opposes accepting it, fears that the social control element will dominate.

The same ethical concerns apply to co-optation, in its "negative" usage, as to the other tactic/techniques described in this section.

Despite the temporal or even long-term pleasures that may be associated with the process of seduction, it is, as a conflict tactic, in all its various guises, outside the usual acceptable norms that apply to rule-regulated conflict.

Emotional "Extortion"

Emotional extortion is most commonly employed in personal-type conflicts (at work or elsewhere). As a tactic, it may rely on the greater "attractiveness" of one of the parties in a social exchange relationship, or on the ability of a participant to generate guilt in others. When attractiveness is the source of control, the very threat of withdrawing from a relationship may serve as a potent means of exercising influence, and "extorting" compliance.

The stimulation of guilt in another person, as a mode of influence, is not an uncommon form of "emotional blackmail." It is likely to occur in close primary relationships, or where there is a strong collective bond among members of a group or organization (e.g., concern about "letting the side down"). Creation of guilt is frequently based on the premise of an unfulfilled obligation in a relationship, that is, an "incomplete exchange." For instance, a person may charge another individual with ingratitude in an attempt to influence that individual's behavior. And the greater the cost of the claimed "sacrifice" on the part of one party, the greater is likely to be the obligation: With the ability to "impose" an obligation goes the potential for control.[2]

Although the "calling in of debts" is, within limits, a normal and acceptable means of gaining an objective, it may transcend the bounds of ethical and legitimate behavior when it reaches the point of emotional extortion.

Divide and Conquer

A commonly employed and frequently manipulative tactic is to divide and conquer, that is, splitting the solidarity of the membership of an opposing group. However, there is a legitimate place in conflict situations for identifying, and even capitalizing on, genuinely divergent goals and interests within the ranks of one's adversaries. It is when the tactic of deceit is combined with that of divide and conquer that it is likely to become truly manipulative.

Pause for Reflection

A number of the tactics discussed in this chapter are employed in the following scenario. The use of such a tactic is denoted by an asterisk. See if you can identify the tactics.

CHANGE AND CONFLICT AT THE SOUTH SIDE
FAMILY AND CHILDREN'S AGENCY

The Agency is funded by voluntary contributions, an endowment administered by the granting foundation, client fees, and limited governmental payments for "purchased" services. It is well established in the community and provides a broad range of family and children's services. The staff consists of a director, 25 workers from various of the helping professions, the business manager, and 8 support staff.

After a six-month search by a selection committee of the Board of Directors, a replacement was appointed for the long-serving former director, who had died on the job. The new executive came highly recommended as being one of the new breed of sophisticated administrators with a strong orientation toward technical efficiency, economic rationality, and accountability. During the selection process the members of the committee were led to believe that the prospective director believed in "maximum feasible participation" by staff in all aspects of organizational decision making. Upon appointment, the new director was permitted to select a deputy from outside the agency.

Shortly after assuming the position, the director made it quite clear that "maximum feasible participation" implied decision making by the "responsible and the competent." In practice this meant that the basic administrative decisions and policy recommendations to the board would be the prerogative of the executive.

The previous executive committee, consisting of the former director, the three supervisors of the major functional units, the business manager, two elected professional staff, and one elected member of the support staff, was dissolved.

In the place of this executive committee, the director announced the formation of an "Executive Advisory Committee" that would play a "vital role" in the decision-making process.* This new advisory committee was to consist of the director, the new hand-picked deputy, the business manager, the three supervisors, and one member of the professional staff selected by the director.* The advisory committee would meet at the pleasure of the director. During the first six months of the new director's months of tenure, the committee met twice, both times in the director's large office.*

The director informed the supervisors that they would be receiving a salary increase and that they could count on support for their decisions from the "top."* It was suggested to the supervisors that they meet monthly with the workers in their respective units and that the workers be encouraged to make suggestions for improving the efficiency of the agency.

It should be noted that these changes in the decision-making process took place in the context of an increasingly conservative social climate.

The professional and support staffs (below the level of supervisor), through their elected spokespersons, expressed objections to the new decision-making procedures, claiming that they were "authoritarian."

They requested a meeting to discuss the matter. In response, the director asked the staff to appoint two of its members to attend a meeting at which their concerns would be discussed.

The meeting was held in the board's conference room, with the director in the chair, flanked by the vice president of the board, the deputy director, the business manager, and the three supervisors.* The director opened the meeting by expressing pleasure at the attendance by the two staff representatives. This was followed by a statement by the director (with the vice president of the board nodding in apparent agreement) that the previous system has been replaced because that type of so-called industrial democracy was inefficient, inappropriate, and violated the principle that decisions should be made by those most qualified to make them.

The staff representatives then were invited to comment or ask questions. After they finished doing so, a few minutes of general discussion followed, during which all the other participants (except the staff representatives) supported the director. The director then indicated that it was good to have had various views aired and that there was overwhelming support for the new procedures. The director then closed the meeting in a friendly manner, shaking hands with the various participants.*

The staff representatives left the meeting convinced that overt resistance would be too risky and probably unsuccessful. At a secret evening meeting of the staff, held in the home of one of them, it was decided that a covert campaign of resistance would be undertaken. This was to include a private meeting with the head of the foundation that provides the endowment, the instigating of a critical letter-writing campaign by members of "client" groups in the community, the leaking of an audio tape (the staff representatives had secretly taped the meeting for a prominent "liberal" member of the board, and a slow-down in work (unofficially reducing the number of clients to be seen).* In addition, a friendly newspaper reporter was to be tipped off and given the material for a story.*

This, then, is the end of the scenario. The eventual outcome? Well, that will be left to your imagination.

SUMMARY

All of the approaches discussed in this chapter have been of a covert and a sometimes subterranean character. They included the strategies of passive resistance or concealment and manipulation, and their associated tactics.

NOTES

1. This definition is a variation on Selznicks, cited in Gamson (1968, p. 135).
2. For an interesting discussion of some of the obligatory and control aspects of exchange relationships among intimates, see Davis (1975, chap 5).

Chapter 6

EMERGENT AGREEMENT

In the conflict management mode discussed in the previous chapter on covert means, the participants were reluctant or unable to engage in overt, rule-structured conflict management. They perceived each other, through a filter of suspicion, as uncooperative or dangerous adversaries, rather than as well-intentioned opponents.

The behavior of the participants using the mode of "Conflict Management by Emergent Agreement" stands in marked contrast to the way in which the participants employing covert means conduct themselves. We now observe opponents whose approach to managing conflict is controlled, and even relatively "gentle." They perceive their mutual interests as likely to be best served by the kind of agreement that emerges from a "collaborative" stance toward conflict management.

These participants use rule-regulated strategy/tactics. Sometimes the rules are contained in explicit agreements. An example of this would be a formal decision to set up a task force, including representatives of both of the conflicting parties, to engage in a joint problem-solving exercise. But, in other circumstances, the rules may simply be generally understood norms or conventions. Illustrative of this would be adherence to "honesty" in efforts to persuade one's opponent as to the wisdom of an argument. In both situations the interaction is quite rule-structured, even though in the one case the rules are explicit and in the other they are implicit.

The strategy and tactics employed in the mode under discussion involve either one-on-one or representational conflict transactions. For instance, you and a colleague may try to persuade each other in a discussion as to the correctness of your respective views on abortion policy. This would be a one-on-one interaction. However, in another circumstance you and the colleague may be advocates for your respective organization's policies—this would be a representational transaction.

The *strategy* to be discussed, within the mode of conflict management by emergent agreement, is "coactive disputation." This strategy encompasses the *tactics* of joint problem-solving, fact-finding, gentle persuasion, and consensual decision making.

COACTIVE DISPUTATION[1]

The selection of this strategic option implies that although there is a dispute between the parties, they are willing to employ cooperative means in confronting their differences and in trying to work out a solution that is reasonably satisfying to both of them. This suggests that the issues at stake are not likely to be of extreme intensity, and that there has not been a "freezing" of commitments by the adversaries. In addition, there may well be an underlying assumption of "rationality" in respect to the likely behavior of the contenders. In other words, it is thought unlikely that oppositional activities, such as coercion, will prove necessary in order to resolve the matters in dispute in an acceptable manner.

Joint Problem-Solving

This tactic requires the contending parties to acknowledge that the issue in dispute constitutes a problem for both, and that they should "put their heads together" to see how it might be overcome. The use of problem-solving is most likely when neither of the participants is really satisfied with existing proposals or positions, but no preferable alternatives are immediately at hand. In some instances, the participants may engage in problem-solving from the time the difficulty is initially recognized, while in other situations a "harder," more adversarial approach may have been tried originally but then converted into that of problem-solving.

An example of the latter sequence was when changes in the structure of the curriculum of a professional school were necessitated by a budgetary cut. The first proposals for modification advanced by the faculty were rejected by the students. After initial, sharply antagonistic discussion, it became clear that staff members were also less than enthusiastic about the preliminary suggestions for altering the curriculum. After this was recognized, and the reality of the pending reduction in funding was accepted by all parties, a joint problem-solving tactic was adopted. This change in approach necessitated the student representatives convincing their constituency that the modification in tactics was not a "sell-out," nor were they being "co-opted."

The difficulty faced by the representatives of the students in this situation is not unusual, and the fact that there was a team of students (rather than one representative) helped because they could vouch for each other's integrity and the correctness of the decision to change the approach. One important value of using multiple representatives in a conflict situation is that the members of the teams can serve as "watchdogs" for each other, thus helping to provide legitimacy as to both the process and the outcome.

On some occasions a third party, a consultant, may be brought in to assist in the process. If this is done as part of a problem-solving tactic, it is imperative that the use of the consultant be appropriate for this function, rather than serving, for instance, as a "reinforcement" for one of the competing parties.

Fact-Finding

Fact-finding may be used as a tactic in itself, or as a technique within another tactical approach. In the first instance, one of the participants may believe that the disagreement about which a conflict revolves is due to inadequate or incorrect data, hence fact-finding might be the appropriate tactic to use. The second use of fact-finding as a technique may be as one aspect of such tactics as problem-solving or negotiation. It may even be the primary activity for one of the third-party roles (ombudsman).

Gentle Persuasion

In terms of the distinction already made between influence and power, this tactic falls on the side of influence. *Persuasion* may be defined as a social process through which one party attempts to affect the actions or ideas of another by means of communicating arguments or appeals.[2] The term suggests efforts being made to convince, to "win over the other side," rather than to outwit or harm one's adversary.[3] There is the further implication that the techniques of persuasion will be oriented toward reason and understanding, rather than toward reward inducement or forced compliance. Persuasion is also usually perceived as being a gradual process rather than resulting in a sudden "conversion." By adding the adjective *gentle* to describe the tactic, we are further distancing it from a "hard-sell" approach.

Gentle persuasion is a "low-pressure" option that is compatible with what Middleman and Goldberg (1974, p. 50) refer to as "the principle of least contest"—that is, the wisdom of beginning with the mildest tactic congruent with the situation.[4] A correlate of its "low-pressure" characteristic is that it tends to be relatively free from the element of threat.[5] For these reasons gentle persuasion is a low-risk tactic that is particularly suitable for use in clashes between intimates, as well as being appropriate in many impersonal conflict situations.

There has been much discussion in the literature as to the factors that contribute to success in the general realm of persuasion. Gamson (1968, pp. 102-103) stresses three primary persuasion resources: skill in communications (writing and speaking), a positive reputation, and personal attractiveness on the part of the influencer.[6] Other relevant competencies include understanding of self and others, self-discipline, and versatility in behavioral styles.[7]

The degree of receptivity to persuasion varies not only with the issue and presentation, but also with time and place. In picking the right moment one has to take into account such transient factors as "moods," as well as more general considerations. For example, if an intellectual/psychological difficulty arises that makes a person question her or his usual way of thinking, there might well be an increased responsiveness on that individual's part to the introduction of different ideas or behaviors.

This is particularly likely during a period of crisis in which one faces new or unanticipated circumstances, or in which there is social alienation or a questioning of ones identity or roles (Schein, 1973, pp. 517-527; Strauss, 1973, pp. 548-558). At such times there is an increased potential for a *redefinition of situations* and even "conversion." By *conversion* I mean a sudden or major reversal of beliefs by an opponent, accompanied by adoption of a different viewpoint. It might be added that the conversion process usually has a strong emotional component, in addition to any intellectual argumentation that might have been influential.[8]

Although there is still much to be learned about what creates effectiveness in the process of persuasion, a variety of techniques have been identified as being potentially useful; unfortunately, only some of these have been researched (and then with results that are not always consistent). The following Action Guide offers suggestions drawn from a range of sources for improving the effectiveness of communications, particularly in reference to conflict management.

Action Guide!

Improving the Effectiveness of Communications

(1)   when communicating in conflict situations:
    (a) check out inferences and assumptions
    (b) amplify unduly subtle messages

    (c) temper overly intense or potentially threatening messages

    (d) converse in the "idiom" of the other party

    (e) make certain that nonverbal communications are consistent with verbal ones

    (f) convey to the other parties the conviction that they have been heard and understood

(2) provide positive reinforcement for ideas and behaviors that support movement in the desired direction

(3) work toward getting the other party to accept your "definition of the situation"

(4) recognize areas of validity in your opponent's position

(5) highlight mutually held principles and invoke opponent's commitment to them without creating undue defensiveness

(6) link areas of agreement to those about which there is still disagreement

(7) stress joint benefits flowing from a change in the direction of the desired position by emphasizing complimentary interests and desired values and norms

(8) build trust and credibility

(9) be consistent

(10) display confidence and autonomy (independence of judgment and attitudes without appearing to be either domineering or unduly prone to compromise)

(11) set an example by "modeling"

(12) remember, in making a presentation:

    (a) the presentation of both sides of an issue appears to be more effective than a single-sided approach (although this may not always be the case if the audience is very poorly informed or uneducated)

    (b) if you discuss both sides of an issue, it is often most effective to present the preferred view last

    (c) the beginning and end of a presentation tend to be remembered longer, with the end being particularly well retained if the argument is an unfamiliar one

    (d) conclusions should be made explicit rather than remaining implicit

    (e) repetition of a message, if not carried to an extreme, tends to increase learning and acceptance

    (f) a message that initially arouses a "need," and then suggest how it might be satisfied, tends to be better remembered as long as the need-arousing is not perceived as threatening

    (g) if it is necessary to provide two messages, one of which is desirable and the other undesirable from the audience's point of view, the desirable one should be presented first

    (h) the effect of a communication is generally greatest soon after exposure

---

In considering various tactics and techniques, it is important to keep in mind that too much perceived pressure may arouse a negative response toward the goal of the persuader, and to the persuader as a person. This reaction is referred to by social psychologists as "reactance" (Feld & Radin, 1982, p. 200).

It may be possible systematically to develop resistance, that is, an "inoculation," against being influenced (Karrass, 1979).[9] Although the research findings in this area are still limited, there does seem to be a basis for arguing that some ways of developing resistance to persuasion are considerably more effective than others. For instance, prior consideration of arguments likely to be used by one's opponents and rehearsal of counterarguments, may prove useful in this regard.

Keep in mind that persuasion can be used not only to resolve conflicts but also to generate conflict, or even to prevent conflict.

Consensual Decision Making

In some situations a consensus emerges from a situation initially characterized by divergent and conflicting commitments. The attempt to produce such a result—that is, a consensus—may be employed as a deliberate tactic in conflict management.

At its best, the use of consensual decision making approximates creative problem-solving; at its worst, it can be manipulative and coercive. The use of consensus as a way of arriving at a decision is often available as an *option* in meetings; however, in some organizations or situations, consensus is a *requirement* (compulsory consensus) if a decision is to be reached. Examples of this are found in some categories of jury trials in given legal systems, and in certain ideologically oriented groups (some collectives).

One of the major advantages of consensual decision making, when used properly, is that it may lead to greater involvement and education of those present. It may stimulate a fuller exploration of the issues and divergent viewpoints, and greater inclusion of "deviants" in the discussion, than when majority decision making is employed. Also, it often tempers the competitive-conflictual element in disputations. It is less likely that there will be a result in which there is a victorious majority and a wounded minority.[10] In some societies, particularly of a traditional type, voting is frowned upon because of its conflict potential—as some human service workers engaged in cross cultural projects discover to their surprise and chagrin.

Research has been done on the outcome of consensual decision making. A number of laboratory studies found that "consensual groups" produce decisions of higher quality, with less emphasis on personal orientations, than do groups using a majority rule. There was one study, though, that concluded that when a group has to choose among various options, of which *only one* is correct, "majority rule will give more reliable decisions in that the decision will be correct more of the time" (Hare, 1976, p. 345). Also, the effects of compulsory consensus, in the sense of a rule of unanimity, have been examined in relationship to the decision-making behaviors of juries. Two of the interesting findings were that the unanimity rule resulted in more equitable participation in the deliberations than did the majority rule, but that it also generated more final agreements,

agreements that may have been "pressured" in some instances (Saks & Hastie, 1978, p. 85).

Despite the positive aspects of consensual decision making, there are serious questions as to its use. It appears to work best in situations in which there are no sharp clashes of interests or principles, and in which all parties are eager to solve the problem. There is also reason to believe it is most effective in small, relatively homogeneous or ideologically motivated groups.

The consensual approach does not seem equally appropriate in formalized or intense forms of negotiation, or in power-oriented conflicts.[11] There is a real danger that the pressure for consensus will be associated with a drive toward conformity-uniformity. This is particularly likely in highly cohesive groups (Collins & Guetzkow, 1964, p. 181).

To conclude: While consensual decision making is a perfectly appropriate and useful tactic in some situations, it is often inapplicable to those forms of conflict in which there are significant disagreements based on commitments or interests. The use of the consensual approach in such circumstances runs the risk of a "manipulated" agreement, or a "masking" of genuine conflictual elements (false consensus). A related result may be that important minority or deviant views get "homogenized," and fail to have the impact that they deserve, particularly in the longer term.

SUMMARY

In this chapter we described a rule-regulated "collaborative" approach to conflict management designated "conflict management by emergent agreement." This mode of managing conflict can be contrasted with the covert means discussed in the prior chapter.

NOTES

1. This strategic category is similar to the mode of intervention referred to as "collaborative" by Brager and Holloway (1978, pp. 131-132). However, we prefer a designation that provides a greater sense of a degree of conflict than is suggested by "collaborative," even though there may be considerable cooperation in managing the conflict.

2. The emphasis on influencing as an interactional process, rather than as the expression of individual capacities, is important: It shifts the focus from question as to "*what* influence individuals have on one another to *how* they influence one another" (Danziger, 1976, p. xvi).

3. Rapoport (1960, p. 11) uses the term *debate* to refer to the "ways of persuasion"; however, we do not use his differentiation between argument (i.e., examination of facts and the chain of logical consequences) and debate (p. 273).

4. Although Middleman and Goldberg (1974, p. 50) use the principle in relation to the worker accomplishing the client task, it can obviously be broadened in its application.

5. Some writers differentiate persuasion from coercion primarily in terms of the amount and type of pressure exerted.

6. Also see Karrass (1979, p. 80).

7. For a discussion of "social styles," see Merrill and Reid (1981, chap. 4).

8. For a discussion of "conversion," particularly as a response to "nonviolent action," see Sharp (1971, pp. 547-549).

9. For additional reading concerning resistance to persuasion, see Freedman et al. (1970, pp. 289-295) and Itamachek (1982, pp. 118-122).

10. Some of the techniques used to reach a "constructive consensus" by the Quakers have been discussed by Stuart A. Chase and are cited in Bernard et al. (1957, pp. 104-106). Other requirements for and advantages of consensual decision making are discussed by Shuts (1973, pp. 294-345).

11. For further discussion of possible limitations of the consensual approach, see Bernard et al. (1957, pp. 106-109).

Chapter 7

DIRECTLY NEGOTIATED AGREEMENT
Introductory Considerations
and Preliminary Phases

One of the processes most popularly associated with conflict management is negotiation. It is to this mode of managing conflict that we now turn. In this chapter the topic will be opened up and explored in an introductory manner, with further development and elaboration in the subsequent chapter.

NEGOTIATION: MEANINGS
AND CENTRAL CHARACTERISTICS

In recent years the social/behavioral sciences, and allied professions, have paid considerable attention to the subject of negotiation. This intensified interest has produced a formidable literature on the topic. Within this very expansive arena we have selected a particular focus on negotiation, that is, negotiation as one strategy in the management of conflicts arising from disputes involving interests and commitments.

Even within the constraints of this focus there will be no dearth of richness in the texture of the unfolding drama of negotiation.

MEANINGS

Negotiation and Bargaining

In our usage, *negotiation* refers to the strategic process through which adversaries try to come to terms, that is, to reach an agreement on matters in which they are in conflict.[1] It encompasses all the transactions in the process, ranging from defining the dispute to its final outcome (Gulliver, 1979, p. 71).

A question that immediately arises is the relationship of *negotiation* to *bargaining*. Although some writers equate the two terms, we shall side with those who distinguish between them. By so doing it is easier to highlight certain of the subprocesses that fall within the framework of negotiation.

Negotiation is a more inclusive concept than bargaining: Negotiation is a *strategic* process, while bargaining is a "broad-spectrum" *tactic* commonly employed within negotiations—particularly, but not exclusively, as part of the *distributive substrategy*. Bargaining is concerned with the give and take, the moves and countermoves, and the use of "carrots" and "big sticks" in hammering out actual agreements. It is often employed in connection with the granting and receiving of concessions.

Bargaining is not the only tactic employed in negotiations. For instance, the invention of "superordinate" solutions—that is, the creation of new, mutually advantageous options—and "debate," which is designed to convince opponents of the correctness of your arguments, perceptions, or courses of action, are other *tactics* involved in negotiations.[2] We shall, in later sections, expand upon these tactics.

The Distributive and the Integrative Substrategies

There are two major approaches to negotiating agreements: the *distributive* and the *integrative*. We consider them to be *substrategies* that share elements and dynamics, as well as possessing differentiating characteristics. This way of "packaging" the two approaches makes up in usefulness for whatever it may lack in conceptual neatness.

The distributive substrategy[3] is based on the assumption that opposing goals, interests, or preferences are at stake and that the most effective method of attaining one's objectives is to try to secure concessions from the other party, while, at least implicitly, being willing to grant some to the opponent. Of course, each of the adversaries is likely to want to get the best or most useful "deal" possible from the other side. Hence the goal is usually to gain more (quantitatively or qualitatively) advantages than one gives.

The integrative substrategy, most simply, may be viewed as an approach that emphasizes negotiating outcomes that are mutually advantageous, although not necessarily of equal benefit to both parties. It stresses problem-solving and the creative development of new solutions. Two important prerequisites for integrative agreements are mutual recognition of a problem involving the interests of both parties that requires a solution, and the necessity for new options incorporating both their interests

(Kreisberg, 1982, p. 223). There is, obviously, a close relationship between this approach and coactive disputation, which was discussed earlier in the book. However, the integrative substrategy occurs within the context of a negotiating transaction. Both of these substrategies, and the differences and similarities between them, will be elaborated upon later.

GENERAL CHARACTERISTICS
OF THE NEGOTIATING PROCESS

Structure and Rule-Regulation

Negotiations may be conducted in formal or informal settings, although "classic" negotiations are usually thought of as being associated with highly organized formats. When the negotiating transactions take place in formalized circumstances, they tend to be characterized by explicit procedures and established norms. Examples of such negotiations are labor-management sessions and meetings set up to try to agree on reductions in nuclear weapons. Even in high-level "summit conferences," though, unplanned informal sessions may well be interspersed with the formalized ones.

By way of contrast, consider an informal, unstructured situation involving "implicit" negotiations between a husband and wife trying to iron out their differences as to vacation plans. The interaction in this type of situation is not likely to be articulated in terms of negotiations, although that is really what is taking place.

Illustrative of a negotiating exchange falling between these two sharply contrasting examples (highly structured and unstructured) is the transaction between a human service worker and a nonvoluntary client involving an effort by the client to get a relaxation of parole conditions. Still another instance of quasi-formalized negotiations is the interaction between a worker and a client in working out a so-called contract that is to guide their interaction in a "helping" situation.

Two normative aspects of negotiations should be elaborated upon. One is that the negotiating relationship is, in a sense, a "voluntary" and "cooperative" one, although it must be noted that the disputants may have been forced by events to enter the process. Participation in a negotiating situation implies that the parties joined in the process because it appeared to be more desirable, in terms of potential outcomes, than nonparticipation (Rubin & Brown, 1975, p. 7).

The "rules of the game" are a second aspect of the normative side of negotiations. Such rules, though, may be fluid and not clearly understood or explicitly worked out. An example of the sometimes tenuous nature of the "rules" would be negotiations with a terrorist holding hostages. These may develop as the negotiating situation evolves. In this sense, the norms governing certain types of negotiation may themselves be an "emergent and fluid product of bargaining interaction" (Bacharach & Lawler, 1981, p. 108).

Categories of Interaction

The participants in formalized negotiations most commonly function in a representational manner. However, at this point we need to add a distinction to those already explicated. We will divide representational interactions into those that are *symmetrical* and those that are *asymmetrical*. The symmetrical ones are those in which both of the participants in the conflict represent constituencies. In the asymmetrical transactions, only one of the actors is functioning in a representational manner, since the other party is acting solely on behalf of him- or herself.

Examples of symmetrical representational transactions are the negotiations between union and management representatives, between students and faculty spokespersons, or between the executives of two agencies involved in a functional territorial dispute. However, the administrator who is negotiating the terms of employment with a nonunionized employee would be functioning within the framework of an asymmetrical representational transaction. The reason for defining this as asymmetrical is that the administrator represents the agency while the potential new worker is acting only on behalf of self. Many worker-client negotiations are also of this character.

Negotiations may also involve one-on-one interactions. Two workers trying to negotiate their differences over the use of a secretary might well fit this category. So too would our previous example of a husband and a wife "implicitly" negotiating their conflicting "wants" over how to spend their vacation time.

Negotiations also play a vital part in third-party interactions. For instance, a mediator frequently negotiates with both of the adversaries, separately or jointly, as well as encouraging them to negotiate with each other.

Negotiations can occur within any of the interactional categories, but the type of interaction may have important consequence for the way in which the negotiations are conducted. This point will be elaborated upon in a subsequent chapter.

Power and Influence

Power is a permeating aspect of the negotiating process. Although influence plays a significant part in negotiations, power is of particular importance, especially in respect to the bargaining that characterizes "distributive" negotiations. And power and tactics are closely linked (Bacharach & Lawler, 1981, p. x, 47). As we shall see, power is a key determinant of bargaining tactics, while, in turn, the choice and use of given tactics often alters the power balance and thus subsequent tactics.

All or any of the power and influence resources discussed earlier in the book may be activated in the process of negotiations.

Communication

Negotiation obviously requires communication. Such communication may be explicit, implicit, or both. Hence communication is a core subprocess within the negotiating context. In thinking about communication, one has to take into account not only the mechanism of communications, and the clarity and techniques of the process, but also the content of the messages being sent and received.

A currently popular notion is that communication difficulties are the source of most of the conflicts in the world, and that good communication skills are a panacea for such disputes. The evidence does not appear to support this apparently reassuring notion. Like most simple explanations of social phenomena, it appears to be more myth than reality.[4] For instance, clarity in a communication that conveys strong antagonism may make matters much worse than if, because of obscurity in the message, the degree of dislike was tempered or hidden. Thus a lack of clarity (or even lack of communication) may sometimes have a positive effect on interpersonal transactions, including those involving negotiation.

Drawing upon what is known, descriptively, about the nature and impact of communications, we move to the level of suggesting some behaviors in the following Action Guide.

Action Guide!

Communication Hints for the Wary Negotiator

(1) Carefully assess how much information should be communicated to the other party in respect to one's own motives and preference. Too much information might expose and thus weaken one's own position. Too little information might slow down negotiations and impede the possibility of reaching a desired outcome. The decision as to what, and how much, information be conveyed should be based not only on one's own preference but also on the perception of the opponent's behavior.

(2) Resist the temptation to withdraw from communicating with your adversaries. Communicational isolation, whatever its cause, tends to increase mistrust and suspicion.

(3) Avoid communication overload in a situation in which there is a marked degree of ambiguity. Excessive communications in such situations may greatly intensify conflict.

(4) Encourage instructions by authoritative third parties that provide information about the availability of communication opportunities and ways in which communication may be used advantageously. This information, combined with pressure to so use the communication opportunities, is likely to have a positive impact on the negotiating process.

(5) Be careful! Remember that the communication of threats tends to increase conflict and reduce the likelihood of agreement. This is particularly the case when the threatening party has a high coercive capacity.

(6) Don't forget that the establishment of credibility is a vital factor in the use of either rewards or threats in bargaining communications.

(7) In your negotiations, take into account the likelihood that suspicious bargainers will communicate more lies and threats but less information than trusting contenders.

(8) Keep in mind that if the opportunities for spoken communication are seriously interfered with, negotiating effectiveness is likely to be impaired.

The Setting

The physical and social-psychological arrangement of the negotiating arena can have a decisive impact on the interactional process. Most important is the creation of a setting that facilitates good communication. However, other considerations must also be given attention in setting the stage for the negotiations. Among these are such matters as seating patterns that symbolize status relationships, "creature comforts," and access to facilities.[5] Even the location of restrooms, and the opportunity to avail oneself of them during negotiating sessions, may have a significant impact on the outcome. Other considerations include the symbolic meaning of a site, access to transportation, privacy or openness, facilities for persons with disabilities, and the austerity or lavishness of the location. Physical arrangements not only influence the atmosphere but may equally serve as clues to the relationship between the contenders.[6]

In an earlier chapter we mentioned that there are research findings indicating that negotiators are likely to be more assertive when on their home ground. Thus in some situations there may be a distinct advantage in negotiating within one's own territory.[7] However, this is by no means an inflexible guideline. For example, if you anticipate the possibility of a "walk out" during negotiations, it is easier to pull this off if the transaction is taking place on the other person's home ground. In some circumstances, the willingness to meet in your opponent's building or office may be seen as a positive gesture of good faith and interest in a productive outcome. Hence in given contexts such a move might be tactically desirable. Another situation in which the willingness to be the "guest" might prove useful is when a superordinate person (e.g., a supervisor or employer) does this in order to reduce the status inequality in the relationship. Finally, in some negotiations it might be very important to choose a neutral site; as a matter of fact, this may well be a prerequisite for the participation of one or the other of the contenders in the transaction.

Timing

Another general consideration is that of time and timing. The skillful use of time and timing can be of marked importance in the process of negotiation. For example, research findings suggest "time pressures increase the likelihood of agreement and tend to be reflected in reductions in bargaining aspirations, demands, and the amount of bluffing that occurs."[8] Also, the timing of interjections can be critical. Of importance as well is the placement of agenda items in terms of the sequencing of topics, the mood and alertness of the participants, and the likelihood of some of the contenders having to withdraw from the meeting at a given time.

One final earthy comment about timing: It is good practice for participants in negotiating sessions to take advantage of available opportunities for rest, food, and the use of toilet facilities.

Audiences

We have already identified audiences as one of the categories of participants in conflict situations. *Audience* was defined as those persons who are "present, physically or psychologically, at the site of conflict/management interaction." It was also pointed out that an audience may be composed of constituents, potential partisans (those affected by the proceedings in some way, even if they don't actively perceive the situation in this manner or try to influence it), and observers. We further alluded to the potential influence of audiences on such strategies of conflict management as negotiations.

No one seriously doubts that audiences can have an impact on the contenders in a struggle. Even in such a rule-regulated, stylized conflict as a football game, the audience is often considered one of the real advantages possessed by the home side. In some football (gridiron) matches, the crowd (audience) has even been referred to as the "twelfth member" of the home team. And it is not only in sports that the audience can have an important affect on a conflict.

Negotiations provide another arena in which audiences can get into the act. However, the influence of audiences on such transactions is often relatively indirect, subtle, and "quiet." Of course, not all audiences have the same type or degree of impact. Among the factors that affect the consequences of audiences are whether or not they are physically present, size and composition, their stake in the outcome, and the audiences' readiness to put pressure on the negotiators (Rubin & Brown, 1975, pp. 43-44).

Although systematic research on the impact of audiences on negotiators and the negotiating process is limited, the findings that do exist suggest the following (pp. 44-53):

(1) The presence (including psychological presence) of an audience, particularly if it is an important or dependent one (e.g., constituent or potential partisan), puts pressure on the negotiator to make a good showing.
   (a) An emphasis by the negotiator on saving face and retaliating may be encouraged by feedback from the audience, as well as by concern as to the impression created on the opponents (the opponent, then, is a type of audience).
   (b) Feedback from an audience suggesting that the negotiator "looks bad" is likely to increase retaliatory behavior toward opponents by that negotiator.
(2) Audiences with a stake in the outcome tend to generate pressures on "their" negotiator toward loyalty, commitment, and advocacy of the audience's preferred positions.
   (a) Even the expectation by a negotiator of a forthcoming meeting with a constituent audience is likely to increase the negotiator's responsiveness to accountability pressures from that audience.
   (b) Increased accountability pressures (perceived or actual) are likely to increase the negotiator's "demandingness" and competitiveness.
   (c) Although a strong sense of commitment to, and identification with, a constituent audience may have positive results, it also has the potential danger of "narrowing the vision" of the negotiator by lessening an awareness of alternatives and putting constraints on the freedom to select from a wider range of options.

The fact that audiences can and do influence the course of the negotiating process suggests that serious attention be given to decisions as to if and when negotiating sessions should be open or closed. An audience does not have to be in physical proximity to the negotiators to have an effect. There is a trend to have meetings of public decision-making bodies open to audiences (live or by TV). Examples would be city council meetings, faculty meetings, congressional/parliamentary sessions, and even courtrooms. Thus far, however, most international negotiations are conducted in closed settings.

There is probably no reliable general guide that can be offered as to whether given negotiations should take place with or without an audience.

A good case can be made for most meetings of ongoing decision-making bodies, in public organizations, to be open. Subordinate recommending units (e.g., committees) differ so greatly in structure and function, though, that no general rule seems to be appropriate. Also, specific negotiating situations vary sufficiently that decisions as to whether to conduct them with or without an audience should probably be made on a case-by-case basis.

In some instances, the "rights" of participants in conflict transactions might be unduly compromised by certain types of public exposure. Hence the televising of criminal proceedings requires further study.

On the basis of present evidence, it does appear to be the better part of wisdom to conduct international negotiations in relatively closed settings. This also appears to be advisable in negotiations with terrorists and comparable situations.

External Stresses

Negotiating when contenders are subject to serious external stresses is not likely to be a good idea. Present evidence suggests that various forms and degrees of stress tend to make the contenders "more rigid, more intolerant of ambiguous situations, more likely to oversimplify the perceptions, and less effective in problem-solving" (Hopmann & Walcott, 1977, p. 303, 321). Thus heightened external stresses and tensions probably tend to be dysfunctional for negotiations, insofar as they are likely to result in greater hostility among the contenders, harder negotiating strategies, and less successful outcomes.

The "moral" of these findings is that it is preferable to be free of stress and rested when undertaking delicate negotiations. However, this may be as difficult to implement as the advice given by some doctors to mothers with small children: "Go home, put your feet up, don't do work around the house or worry about the family."

The Characteristics of the Participants

As previously observed, the personal and group characteristics of the participants in a conflict situation affect the way in which they perform. This certainly seems to be true in the negotiating process. Some suggestive findings as to the impact of the "personal" element in negotiations, flowing from still inconclusive research, are as follows:

(1) Personality factors probably have the greatest impact early in the negotiating process, before structural factors become dominant (Druckman, 1977, p. 30).

(2) The less negotiators are constrained by their constituencies, the more likely that their personalities will influence their perceptions and definitions of the situation (Herman & Kogan, 1977, p. 186).

(3) It appears that persons characterized by a "power orientation and obeisance to others in power, proneness to concrete thinking, and an attitude toward others that is generally suspicious and cynical" are inclined to negotiate in a less cooperative manner than those with fewer of these attributes (Rubin & Brown, 1975, p. 186). Hence power oriented, concrete-minded negotiators may be particularly prone to interpret "accommodating gestures" as a sign of weakness.

(4) Persons with very competitive predispositions tend to be "insensitive to (or uninterested in) interpersonal cues; they do not vary their behavior in response to the other; they misperceive the other's intentions; they underestimate the importance of their own behavior in determining what the other does; they view the world as consisting of others just like themselves" (Rubin & Brown, 1975, p. 185).

(5) Persons who are relatively flexible in their ethical judgments tend to negotiate more cooperatively than those with more extreme and "rigidly" moralistic views (Rubin & Brown, 1975, p. 188).

(6) Persons in low-status or low-power positions (e.g., women, American blacks, etc.) tend to show greater sensitivity and responsiveness to interpersonal cues during negotiations than those with higher power or status (Rubin & Brown, 1975, p. 165).

(7) Persons are more likely to negotiate cooperatively with opponents of the same race than with those of another race (Rubin & Brown, 1975, p. 163).

(8) While men tend to orient themselves to the "impersonal" task of optimizing their gains, women appear to be more reactive to interpersonal aspects of the relationship with their opponents. Thus cooperative or competitive behavior by men and women in negotiating situations appears to be influenced, at least in part, by different orientations and cues (Rubin & Brown, 1975, pp. 172-174).

(9) Negotiators who display marked deference toward the wishes of higher-status persons often behave in an exploitative manner toward opponents of a lower status (Rubin & Brown, 1975, p. 168).

It is important to reiterate that the cited findings should be treated as tentative rather than definitive. Furthermore, personality factors are not discrete elements in the negotiation process; they need to be seen as part of transactions involving a multiplicity of dynamically interacting components. This is the reason some analysts have suggested that, rather than isolating personality characteristics per se, they be studied in interaction with role aspects and situational phenomena (Herman & Kogan, 1977, p. 270).

From the prior descriptive discussion we have derived several suggestions for action.

Action Guide!

(1) Don't passively accept as an accomplished fact a room arrangement that you believe will disadvantage you as a negotiator. You can, without casting doubts on the intentions of the host or adversary, simply indicate that you just don't find the arrangement suitable or comfortable.

(2) Treat the question of whether or not there should be an audience present during negotiations not only as a policy matter but also as a tactical issue. Is it likely to benefit or harm your position in the negotiations—and the process itself?

(3) Take into account the personal characteristics of your adversary and the degree of structure/formality in making your strategic/tactical decisions, as well as choice of techniques. Caution: It is easy to fall into the trap of stereotyping your opponent on the basis of inadequate knowledge. Give your adversary the benefit of the doubt initially, but keep your "powder dry."

Negotiation is but one mode of conflict management. Other strategies may well be employed, either out of preference or out of necessity. Hence, in some disputes, the first obstacle encountered is when one party wishes to negotiate while the opponent prefers another option. The choice of strategies/tactics depends, in large measure, on the parties' perceptions of their chances of success with one approach as compared with an alternative. A weakness in many of the writings on the subject of negotiation is that of underestimating the difficulty of getting agreement to negotiate—and the strong measures that may be required to initiate the negotiating process. In some instances, it may even prove virtually impossible to get the other party into a negotiating situation.

Keeping the above cautionary remarks in mind, we will move into our discussion of the negotiating process. Chart 7.1 should be consulted in association with the subsequent discussion that describes and elaborates the elements depicted in it. The chart breaks the process into two streams, one according to the flow of the distributive substrategy and the other following the movement of the integrative substrategy. The elements of the process depicted in the middle of the chart apply to both options.

In practice, the flow between steps in both options may not all be in one direction—there is sometimes a temporary feedback reversal that alters the sequence. Although the distributive and the integrative are identifiable alternatives, they are by no means totally discrete substrategies. They may overlap and impinge on each other. The tactics commonly associated with one of them may be employed in the other. It is not uncommon for the experienced negotiator to alternate approaches. Despite these reservations, the two substrategies are distinct enough to warrant separate depiction on the chart and in the discussion.

CHART 7.1

Negotiating: The Distributive and Integrative Options, A Flow Chart

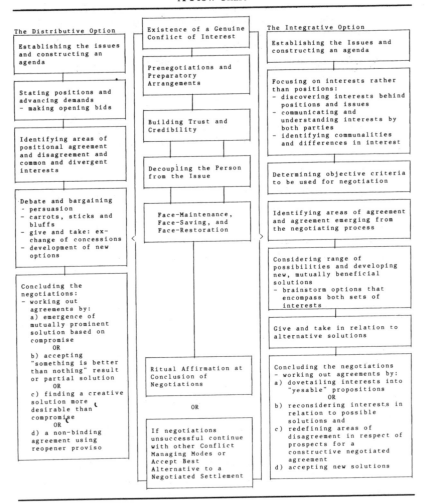

The Distributive Option	Existence of a Genuine Conflict of Interest	The Integrative Option
Establishing the issues and constructing an agenda		Establishing the Issues and constructing an agenda
	Prenegotiations and Preparatory Arrangements	
Stating positions and advancing demands - making opening bids		Focusing on interests rather than positions: - discovering interests behind positions and issues - communicating and understanding interests by both parties - identifying communalities and differences in interest
	Building Trust and Credibility	
Identifying areas of positional agreement and disagreement and common and divergent interests		
	Decoupling the Person from the Issue	Determining objective criteria to be used for negotiation
Debate and bargaining - persuasion - carrots, sticks and bluffs - give and take: exchange of concessions - development of new options	Face-Maintenance, Face-Saving, and Face-Restoration	Identifying areas of agreement and agreement emerging from the negotiating process
		Considering range of possibilities and developing new, mutually beneficial solutions - brainstorm options that encompass both sets of interests
Concluding the negotiations: - working out agreements by: a) emergence of mutually prominent solution based on compromise OR b) accepting "something is better than nothing" result or partial solution OR c) finding a creative solution more desirable than compromise OR d) a non-binding agreement using reopener proviso	Ritual Affirmation at Conclusion of Negotiations OR If negotiations unsuccessful continue with other Conflict Managing Modes or Accept Best Alternative to a Negotiated Settlement	Give and take in relation to alternative solutions Concluding the negotiations - working out agreements by: a) dovetailing interests into "yesable" propositions OR b) reconsidering interests in relation to possible solutions and c) redefining areas of disagreement in respect of prospects for a constructive negotiated agreement d) accepting new solutions

THE PROCESS OF NEGOTIATION: BEGINNING STAGES

PRENEGOTIATIONS: GETTING AGREEMENT TO NEGOTIATE

Negotiations may occur in the early, middle, or late stages of a conflict. The point at which they are initiated can significantly influence the process and outcomes. Regardless of the timing, however, for negotiations to be started each of the contenders must perceive the possibility, if not the likelihood, that an agreement might be reached that would be more desirable (or at least not less desirable) than no such agreement (Deutsch, 1977, p. 216).

Another precondition is that both parties recognize that there is more than one outcome that might be acceptable; this implies a willingness to engage in give and take. The negotiating process involves "mixed motives" on the part of the contenders. Their orientation toward each other is conflictual in regard to interests or goals, but they must possess a sufficiently cooperative motivation to be willing to work together to try to achieve a mutually acceptable outcome (Deutsch, 1977, p. 216). The decision to enter into negotiations should not be thought of as being necessarily based upon calm, rational calculations, or on a desire to be reasonable. In fact, the coercive use of power to raise the potential, or actual, costs of *not negotiating* is frequently necessary in order to achieve an agreement to negotiate.

PREPARATORY ARRANGEMENTS

Once agreement has been reached to proceed with negotiations, various "housekeeping" matters require attention, for instance, selection of the time and place and who will serve as host. Although these may appear to be relatively routine considerations, they raise significant tactical questions, as our prior discussions on setting and timing suggests. This is also very much the case in relation to physical arrangements (e.g., shape of the table, who sits where).

Another aspect of the preliminary arrangements has to do with establishing "ground rules" for the negotiations. These rules include decisions as to which persons and how many will be involved in the negotiations, the meeting procedures, and whether the discussions are to be open or closed.

The preparatory arrangements are usually more formalized when the negotiations are of a representational type. In one-on-one transactions, it may often be necessary to improvise. I know of a situation in which one of the parties in continuing one-on-one negotiations regularly had too much potent liquid refreshment at lunch time, with the result that he became more aggressive and irascible in the afternoon. Hence those who had to negotiate with him would try to do so during the morning hours.

In another instance a human service worker had to negotiate with an involuntary client in that person's backyard, while the client continued to mow the lawn. This was obviously not a preferential site for negotiations, but there was no effective alternative other than relying entirely on court-enforced coercive measures. Hence the negotiations were conducted as the two parties walked back and forth across the lawn, with both the mowing and the conversation proceeding. Despite these unpromising circumstances the negotiations were productive—and when the mowing was completed the worker was invited into the house by the client to continue their discussion over a cup of soup.

There are, of course, many types of informal or even unexpected negotiations in which the participants start negotiations without any preparation. For example, two colleagues may engage in "implicit" negotiations, without any warmup, as to where they should go for lunch. Or, in the midst of a harmonious discussion, a conflict may break out and negotiations may begin quickly without anticipation.

Finally, in asymmetrical negotiations, in which one party is acting in a representational role and the other on a one-on-one basis (e.g., a worker and a client), the one who is serving in the representational capacity (representing the organization) is more likely to make conscious preparations than is the other party.

Inferences as to action-oriented cautions and suggestions may be drawn from the prior discussion. Two of these appear in the following Action Guide.

Action Guide!

(1) Don't assume that an expressed willingness to negotiate means the same thing to the other party as it does to you! Sometimes the acceptance of an offer to negotiate a dispute implies only that one party is agreeing to participate in a discussion, or to hear complaints. The genuineness of an offer to negotiate (in the true sense of the word) may have to be tested once the process is underway. Be careful that any reservations you may have about your adversary's commitment to negotiating doesn't itself impede the process and become a self-fulfilling concern.

(2) Don't despair over an initial refusal to negotiate. Sometimes nothing more than reformulating the issue in dispute produces a change of heart. If not, then the use of rewards or coercive means might so alter the cost/benefit balance as to bring about a willingness to engage in negotiations.

SUMMARY

In this chapter we introduced and depicted the negotiating process, clarified some key concepts, and briefly discussed prenegotiations and preparatory arrangements.

NOTES

1. Our definition is close to that employed by Gulliver (1979, p. xiii).

2. See Rapoport (1960, pp. 8-12) for a discussion of the terms *debate, fight,* and *games.*

3. The term *distributive* is attributed to Walton and McKersie by Pruitt and Lewis (1977, p. 169).

4. For a general discussion of communications in conflict, see Miller and Simons (1974).

5. It is not feasible to discuss all aspects of the physical environment, such as room, color, ventilation, and so forth, but factors of this sort can also significantly influence negotiations.

6. For an interesting discussion of physical arrangements and their significance in negotiation/bargaining, see Rubin and Brown (1975, chap 5).

7. A divergent view is put forth by Fletcher (1983, p. 86).

8. As Rubin and Brown (1975, p. 123) indicate, an interesting point is that in dealing with desperate or irrational people (e.g., terrorist holding hostages), one goal of the negotiation is to protract the bargaining process since time tends to be on the side of a bloodless solution.

Chapter 8

DIRECTLY NEGOTIATED AGREEMENT
The Negotiants Engage

The pulse quickens as the participants prepare to engage one another in the high drama of negotiations. To assist in understanding the unfolding events, a brief excursion into the language of negotiation will be useful.

THE LANGUAGE OF NEGOTIATION

Three terms, commonly employed in discussions of negotiation, are *argument, compromise,* and *concession.*

Argument

Arguments are those "justifications, explanations, or rationalizations" that are offered in support of an approach, suggestion, or position taken by the participants in negotiations (Bacharach & Lawler, 1981, p. 157). They are designed to influence the other party's view of the situation and process.

Compromise

Compromise refers to an agreement based on mutual concessions, arrived at by a give-and-take process.

Concession

By *concession* is meant a "change of offer in the supposed direction of the other party's interest that reduces the level of benefit sought" (Pruitt &

Lewis, 1977, p. 19). It is usually a call for reciprocation (Gulliver, 1979, p. 165). Since concessions are attempts to modify the other party's behavior or perceptions, they are tactical acts. Thus concessions may be thought of as ways of "gaining advantage as much as they are means of giving something to the opponent" (Bacharach & Lawler, 1981, p. 80). *Concession rate* refers to the speed at which concessions are made—thus the time involved in a decline in the demand level (Pruitt & Lewis, 1977, p. 19).

Argument is a vital aspect of the tactic of debate, while compromise and concession are key maneuvers within the bargaining tactic.

In the following discussion of strategic and tactical dynamics, the "model" is that of representational negotiation of a "symmetrical" type. However, much of the content is also applicable to one-on-one and asymmetrical negotiations, be they with colleagues, clients, or "significant others." At various points, particular reference will be made to these other categories of negotiating transactions.

REQUISITES FOR EFFECTIVE NEGOTIATION

No matter which negotiating substrategies or tactics are employed, there are certain behaviors likely to enhance the results. These requisites for effective negotiations are depicted in the middle column of Chart 7.1. Their location is designed to indicate that they are not exclusive to either the distributive or the integrative options.

Building Trust and Credibility

Trust and credibility are vital elements in successful negotiations. They not only reflect perceived characteristics of the negotiators but are also important determinants of the way the negotiations will be conducted. In addition, the presence of mutual trust may contribute greatly to the development of a positive atmosphere for the negotiations. Even in situations involving experienced contenders and hard bargaining, some degree of trust must be present to make the process work. However, while trusting, and being seen as trustworthy, are important elements in satisfactory negotiations, trust is not the same thing as being naive, or as acting on the basis of unquestioning faith. As Deutsch points out, despite some similarities between faith and interpersonal trust, there are important differences: "Faith is more blind than trust; trust is less certain than faith; faith is more closely linked to authoritarian values, while trust is more closely tied to egalitarian values" (Deutsch, 1977, p. 167).

In addition to projecting personal qualities that generate trust, negotiators can also take concrete actions to reinforce this image. Some of these techniques include demonstrating an expectation that the opponent is worthy of trust by a "free offer" (not demanding immediate reciprocal action) or by showing trust in a "minor" matter (e.g., allowing the other party to decide on a suitable site for the first meeting); indicating a genuine concern with the problems the adversary faces in the negotiations; avoiding indiscriminate promises; and offering cues suggesting a willingness to cooperate (Zartman & Herman, 1982, pp. 32-35).

Such actions should not be confused with "pathological trusting"—that is, a "fixed" psychological set toward trusting irrespective of the situation, evidence, or consequences of acting in such a manner (Deutsch, 1977, pp. 169-176). Gullibility, or an undisciplined need to trust the other party because of an intense desire to be liked or approved of, are not the building blocks of that kind of realistic trust required for effective negotiations.

Credibility is related to being perceived of as trustworthy. The emphasis here is on believing that promised actions and outcomes will, in fact, be forthcoming. This involves not only the intention to act in a certain manner, but also the capacity to do so. Credibility is particularly important when associated with threats, promises, claims to be able to act with authority, or the assertion of particular knowledge or competence.

Brager and Holloway (1978, p. 191) make an interesting point when, in linking credibility, prestige, and "attractiveness," they note that perceived expertise may be more influential in technical matters while agreement on values and "attractiveness" may be more important in value-oriented matters. They also note that credibility is often increased by a "soft-sell" approach and by the apparent absence of excessive self-interest. However, caution needs to be applied to the assumed desirability of avoiding the appearance of self-interest.

Most negotiations involve self-interest, to a greater or lesser extent, and the claim that an opponent's position is less credible because of such self-interest may simply be a technique designed to discredit inappropriately that person's demands. The assertion of self-interest as a charge against another participant is sometimes employed as a form of manipulative "social control." It may be used against human service workers by powerful interests in the community who pose as objective and disinterested societal policy arbiters (e.g., business leaders on governmental bodies or boards of management of voluntary community organizations). Here again, the reader should be reminded of the distinction made earlier in this book between self-interest and selfishness.

Decoupling the Person From the Issue

Since negotiators are people, there is no way in which the negotiating process can be depersonalized in the sense of eliminating emotions and personal characteristics from the transactions. The machinelike negotiator, who is always rational, coldly calculating, consistent, predictable, and devoid of feelings of frustration, anger, and competitiveness, is more a myth than a reality. It is perfectly reasonable and desirable for the contenders in a negotiating situation, as in any other human interaction, to be "emotionally involved" and concerned with the relational aspects of the process. Nevertheless, admonitions such as "don't take it personally" or "separate the person from the problem" are not simply meaningless slogans emanating from ivory tower sources.

There is much that can be done to lessen destructive interpersonal interactions during negotiations without dehumanizing the process. It is important to do so for at least three reasons: The resultant impaired relationships may well interfere with the negotiating process and result in less satisfactory outcomes; future transactions are likely to be more difficult and uncertain; and there may be severe psychological costs for the contenders, including the potential rupturing of gratifying personal relationships. Remember the point made in an earlier chapter: Liking and the perception of agreement tend to be linked, as are the perceptions of disagreement and dislike.

There are various "do's and don'ts" that may assist negotiators in decoupling heated argumentation from the development of interpersonal hostility and aggression. At the level of technique this includes the use of "coffee breaks," or similar intermissions, to emphasize or reinforce existing personal ties. For example, if you typically play tennis or cards with your opponent, discuss the last match or finalize the time for the next one during the break, or, if you both belong to the same social organization, chat about that during the intermission. But a word of caution—this technique requires delicacy in implementation. If done in a heavy-handed or obviously phony fashion it may indeed backfire.

Another bit of advice is to avoid withdrawing from usual interactions with your opponents. There is a pronounced tendency to reduce the amount of social contact with persons with whom one is in a serious dispute. And yet it is often a counterproductive response to the situation. If you go to a movie or to dinner on a regular basis, don't stop doing it during conflictual negotiations, although it may make you feel quite uncomfortable to continue to do so. It is very important to maintain already existing links. Of course, if you wish, for whatever reason, to signal personal disapproval, then such a withdrawal might be used for that purpose. However, if you do so make certain that it really is a disciplined tactic, rather than an "uncontrolled" action arising from anger or discomfort.

Some of the points made above are summarized and given an action focus in the following Action Guide.

Action Guide!

(1) Recognize and accept the legitimacy of highly charged feelings in the reactions of the negotiators (including yourself).
(2) If feelings get too intense, consider taking a break or calling for a cooling-off period.
(3) Calming "self-talk" can sometimes help one keep feelings under control.
(4) Maintain existing personal relationships with your adversary—even if it is difficult.
(5) Don't make the negotiations a personal battle between you and your opponents.
(6) Remember, anger tends to beget anger—try not to respond to emotional attacks in a like manner.
(7) If you think your actions or motives are being misjudged, demonstrate by your behavior what the "real you" is like.
(8) Demonstrate, verbally and nonverbally, that you are concerned about your adversary's feelings and well-being, but avoid patronizing.

All of the preceding action suggestions apply to both representational and one-on-one negotiations. There are additional considerations, though, that come into play in certain one-on-one negotiations and require attention. For instance, in negotiations among friends it is particularly important to make it clear that the *friendship itself is not being negotiated.* And, in worker-client one-on-one negotiations, it is essential that the worker demonstrate personal acceptance and regard, while avoiding excessive promises, building unrealistic expectations, or generating false optimism.

Face-Maintenance, Face-Saving,
and Face-Restoration

Concern about "face" (i.e., dignity or prestige) is not just a quaint characteristic of exotic cultures. It is, in fact, an important consideration in negotiations in most societies, although the emphasis on face may be stronger in some cultures than in others. Certainly, concern about face in its various aspects should be kept very much in mind by any negotiator.

Face-maintenance is the desire of a participant in negotiations to convey an impression of capability and strength. *Face-saving* is preventative, that is, trying to forestall actions that would tend to make one appear to be incompetent, weak, or inadequate. *Face-restoration* refers to attempts to restore the damage done to one's "face" by prior actions; such reactive efforts may range from seeking redress (e.g., apology) to retaliating (e.g., engaging in counter face-attacking actions).[1]

Matters of face often fall within the category of intangible issues, although they may well emerge from negotiating interactions surrounding tangible concerns. In some situations intangible matters of this sort may end up dominating the negotiating process. The bargaining exchange is particularly likely to invoke face-maintenance issues because of the necessity for the negotiators to be simultaneously yielding and firm. Obviously, it is difficult to strike a perfect balance between these two imperatives, and a consequence of errors in this respect may be the loss of face. Analyses of negotiating sessions suggest that the participants often use disclaimers to lessen the likelihood that they will be perceived as weak or incapable. An example of such a precautionary statement is: "I know this statement sounds like we're unprepared, but. . . ."

It may well be in your interest, as a negotiator, to assist your opponent in saving face. Techniques that might be employed to aid your opponent's face-saving requirements include attributing the weaknesses or errors in your adversary's position to forces beyond that person's control (Pruitt & Lewis, 1977, p. 146); giving generous credit to your opponent for her or his ideas and willingness to be reasonable; making your proposals as consistent as possible with your adversary's self-image and principles (Fisher & Ury, 1981, p. 29); and making the other participant look as good as possible in front of her or his constituencies. Remember, a negotiator's unduly hard-line behavior may be an attempt to prevent loss of face. Also, "taking things personally" may really be an expression of the belief that the other's action is a threat to one's self-image. Face-restoration activities include the intensification of personal attacks on the opposing party, raising the "price," "grandstanding," or statements such as "I have been misunderstood," or "you misinterpreted my argument."

The most important element (regulator) in the range of face-maintenance considerations is the opponent. Brown (1975, pp. 283-284) contends that if an opponent creates (intentionally or unintentionally, directly or indirectly) in a person a sense of being unjustly treated (e.g., intimidated), then this is likely to increase that individual's face-maintenance motives and "to call forth specific responses designed to assert or reassert one's capability and strength."

Third parties may also be important regulators of face-maintaining activities. Audience feedback is one such example. Another is the mediator who might well be important in respect to face-saving. Research in this connection indicates that persons who make concessions in accordance with a "mediator's suggestion were apparently able to dispel their feelings of personal weakness by passing much of the responsibility for their concessions on to him."[2] Offensive or defensive actions concerned with the various aspects of face-maintenance can have a great impact on negotiations, and the wise negotiator will take this into account in making comments and in selecting tactics and techniques.

THE DISTRIBUTIVE AND
INTEGRATIVE STRATEGIC OPTIONS

In the previous chapter we briefly described the distributive and integrative substrategies. Now we shall elaborate upon each and highlight their similarities and differences. As one moves into the negotiating process it is useful to make a tentative choice as to which of the substrategic options will be emphasized. The use of the words *tentative* and *emphasize* in the preceding sentence is quite deliberate. It is intended to highlight the fact that one's choice of strategic (and tactical) options is necessarily influenced by the actions of the other participants in the encounter. For instance, if one of the actors insists on negotiating in terms of fixed positions (distributive) rather than interests (integrative), then the distributive strategic option may have to be adopted by both parties.

It is not unusual for the strategic emphasis to alter during the course of the negotiations. Such a shift may have been intended by one or both of the participants from the start, or it may have simply evolved from the interactional dynamics. Let's keep in mind, as well, that the substrategies are not truly discrete (despite contrary views by some). There may well be an interplay and overlap between the two approaches in any given negotiating situation. Certainly, as we shall see, some of the same tactics are employed in both strategic thrusts.

The Distributive Substrategy

The defining characteristic of this strategic option is the distributing of gains/losses through a process of compromise. Involved in such compromises are the gaining and granting of concessions. The gaining of concessions usually requires tactics that make granting concessions appear to be in your adversary's interests (Pruitt, & Lewis, 1977, p. 169).

The distributive approach usually implies a considerable degree of toughness and the use of argument, as well as the employment of other power resources. It often involves the tactic of bargaining—that is, the pitting of positions against one another by the adversaries. The anticipated or hoped-for outcome is that the distance between the demands of the opposing parties will be narrowed through mutual, but not necessarily equal, concessions, thus allowing an agreement to be reached. Some writers refer to the "hard" tactics used in the distributive approach as competitive behavior, since the objective is "to gain an advantage for the self at the other's expense" (Pruitt & Lewis, 1977, p. 15).

An example of the use of the distributive approach in everyday life would be to offer a merchant $75 for a portable stereo radio for which the asking price is $100. When the merchant sticks to the original price, you put on your coat and start to walk out. At that point the seller calls you back, you resume negotiations, and finally the purchase is made for $85. Much labor-management negotiation over the issue of wages and working conditions is conducted along the same lines.

The Integrative Substrategy

The most significant aspect of this strategic option is its emphasis on the development of innovative problem-solving outcomes, based on "merit," which are designed to provide gains for both of the contenders. Merit, of course is not a value-free, "objective" judgment, despite the impression given by some proponents of the integrative substrategy. Within this approach much attention is paid to such tactics as identifying and focusing on the interests, rather than the contending positions, of the adversaries; the use of objective criteria; and the creative invention of mutually beneficial solutions. Although few outcomes are truly equal in their benefits, there are many possibilities for results that provide at least some significant gains (or reduction of costs) for both parties.

One of the reasons for stressing interests, rather than positions, in this strategic approach is that positions tend to be cast in a "frozen" adversarial stance. It is difficult to find room for creative problem-solving and reasoned change when positions are the center of attention. Another rationale for focusing on interests rather than positions is that the contenders usually have multiple interests underlying their positions; some of these interests may be divergent, but others may be shared. For this reason, negotiators, using the integrative strategy, may find more common ground than if they are concerned only with the demands (positions) over which they are seemingly at complete odds.

Although some writers tend to idealize the integrative approach and treat it as a mutually exclusive alternative to the distributive mode, others tend to see the two in less polar terms. For example, even in integrative bargaining there may be concessions and compromises, although there is likely to be more emphasis on searching for, and developing, new outcome possibilities than in the distributive approach (Gulliver, 1979, p. 150). Many negotiations contain elements of both substrategies, but some results are largely distributive, while others tend to be predominately integrative (Kriesberg, 1982, p. 218). However, the integrative mode generally makes less use of hard competitive tactics and requires a greater degree of trust and coordination of goals than does the distributive.

Integrative techniques may take a number of different forms, including putting more "goodies" on the table (broadening the pie), alternating benefits, "logrolling," or securing mutual advantages at the expense of nonparticipants in the negotiations.[3] The first of these implies adding to the "pot" so that there is more to go around, while the second, alternation, allows each party to achieve desired outcomes but at different times (sequential gratifications). Logrolling implies a trade-off of concessions (similar to distributive behavior) in regard to issues of differing importance to the contenders. This allows each of the contending parties to gain in areas of high importance to them. The fourth mechanism is self-evident. It is said that integrative bargaining requires "flexible rigidity," that is, firmness in respect to goals but flexibility as to means.

The advantages of an integrative approach are that the results are likely to be more satisfying to all the concerned parties. And the probable consequence is that there is likely to be a better basis for positive interaction between the contenders in the future. There is a greater probability that the terms of the integrative outcome will be adhered to rather than subverted. In addition, the costs in terms of frustration and antagonism are likely to be minimized. Furthermore, the results of an integrative approach have the potential to be more creative and satisfying. Finally, negotiations conducted in an integrative manner are less likely to end up in a deadlock.[4]

The major drawback of the integrative substrategy is that the issues and interests involved must lend themselves to such an approach if it is to work. In addition, the behavior of the negotiators (and their constituents) might not be compatible with an integrative approach. For example, an adversary who is hard in tactics and goals may create circumstances in which an attempt to use the integrative mode by the other party will be fruitless, or will even make that person vulnerable to exploitation. In such situations, justifiable interests and demands might not be achieved by use of the integrative approach.

The distributive and integrative approaches are appropriate in different circumstances, or even at different times in the same negotiating session. In reality they are, as we have suggested, complex substrategies of negotiation, often with mixed, rather than "pure," characteristics. To give a greater sense of reality to these strategic options, consider the following situation, which closely parallels many actual disputes in the human services:

> The "nonmedical" human service workers (social workers, psychologists, "outreach workers") in a large community health center wanted to be

represented on the Center's board of management. They formed an alliance after the individual occupational groups had their requests for such representation turned down. The board's chairperson agreed to meet with a small delegation from the combined human service workers' alliance, but at that meeting the chairperson simply reiterated the prior opposition to the sought-after representation and refused to negotiate further on the issue. The frustrated alliance then "lobbied" an influential community group that was represented on the board. This led to the president of that community group approaching the chairperson of the board with the firm suggestion that real negotiations with the workers should be initiated. This advice was heeded and negotiations began. After hard bargaining, during which the alliance's request for multiple representatives was scaled down, a "two-step agreement" was worked out. Step one was to be an interim stage, during which the worker's alliance would be granted one place on the board. Step two involved setting up a working party, composed of board and alliance members, with the mandate to bring back recommendations for a possible expansion and restructuring of the board to allow for more members from community groups, as well as additional representatives from the alliance. This proposal had some appeal to the chairperson, who perceived additional community group representation as being possibly advantageous, both as a means of increasing financial support for the center and as a way of "diluting" the influence of any additional alliance representation. The alliance, for its part, saw the working party as a potential means of increasing its representation on the board and was not adverse to additional community members.

What strategies/tactics were employed by the human service workers in the above case history? First, after unsuccessful efforts for representation by the individual occupations, an alliance was formed. Despite the increased power resources this move generated, the workers were still unable to get negotiations started, so they exerted further pressure on the chairperson by getting an influential community group to act on their behalf. This increased the potential "costs" to the chairperson (alienation of an influential community group), who responded to this prospect by agreeing to engage in "good faith" negotiations. The first stage of the agreement (the interim solution) was a clear example of distributive negotiations, while the second stage offered the possibility of a predominately (but not exclusively) integrative outcome that might provide at least some benefits for both parties. This conflict episode is an example of the interplay of the two substrategies and associated tactics and techniques.

We now leave the matter of the major strategic options to turn to the phases of the negotiating process.

THE PHASES OF
THE NEGOTIATING PROCESS

PHASE 1. ESTABLISHING THE ISSUES
AND CONSTRUCTING THE AGENDA

Except in instances of very informal or "implicit" negotiations, it is usual to structure the negotiations by means of an agenda. Certainly, this is a common step in representational types of negotiating. To set up a useful agenda requires, at a minimum, identifying, presenting, and ordering the issues. It is useful, to the extent feasible, to take advantage of the agenda-building phase to explore the underlying interests of the contestants. By clarifying the issues at stake (and their importance), and the interests they reflect, the goals of the parties in the negotiating situation are brought to the surface. This phase of the process is common to both the distributive and the integrative approaches, although the presentation of divergent positions tends to characterize the former, while interests will be stressed in the latter.

The listing and ordering of the issues about which the negotiations are centered may seem like a straightforward exercise. After all, since both parties decided to negotiate, might one not assume that they are in agreement as to the content of the negotiations? Unfortunately, many negotiating situations lack that degree of neatness and precision. Further-more, since the issues to be discussed commonly reflect divergent underlying interests or concerns, there may well be disagreement among the participants on which topics should be included in the discussions, and in what priority order.

Even when the matters-in-dispute that brought about the negotiating situation appear clear-cut, a need for issue specification and further clarification usually emerges once the discussion is underway. This may open up additional areas of complexity and differences that, in turn, stimulate argumentation and require decisions. Although there may be shared interests, and issues about which there is a consensus, others might generate a sharp division of views. Nevertheless, agreement on this preliminary step of issue clarification is essential before the substance of the issues can be systematically addressed.

Gaining acceptance of one's definition of the issues, thus of the situation, is a major tactical event. Among the situation-defining decisions that have to be made are those pertaining to matters to be included and to be excluded, the wording of the issues, the scope and priority given each issue, and questions of issue linkages or disassociation. This process is complicated by the fact that, for reasons of tactical advantage, intensity of feelings, or confusion as to the original specifications, numerous items are likely to be thrown into the "pot" at the beginning, some of which may be of doubtful appropriateness (Gulliver, 1979, p. 127). In fact, a participant may put forward an issue despite recognition that its chances of being included in the negotiations are slim. After all, issues can be used as trading bait.

In some instances, substantive discussions do begin without the competing definitions of the issues having been clarified. While this may be a useful way of preventing an early stalemate, there is the danger that the divergent definitions may lead to later confusion and delays, resulting in serious difficulties in securing a final agreement.

Differences in the beginning of negotiations regarding the definitions, inclusion, and ordering of issues may be resolved in a number of ways. Some issues may be of much less importance to one side than the other, hence there may be little resistance to inclusion of such an item by the party to whom it is a minor matter. In other instances, an issue may be absolutely ruled out by defining it as nonnegotiable. Often, the decisions as to issues, particularly when the distributive option is used, are made through a bargaining process involving trade-offs, increasing or decreasing the scope of the issues, sequencing, or compromises. Also, the very discussion of issues may, through clarification, lead to a redefinition of them that is acceptable to both parties when the integrative option is dominant. Identifying and understanding interests, shared and divergent, is emphasized as a way of getting agreement on the agenda.

There are many issue considerations that can have an important impact on the effectiveness of the negotiating process. Some of these issue-related matters may arise *throughout* the negotiating transaction rather than just in the initial agenda-constructing phase. Nevertheless, for convenience sake, we will discuss them as part of this section, although recognizing that not all issue concerns can be compartmentalized within a given phase of the negotiation process.

Some of the more important of these issue considerations are listed below.

(A) Location of issues on the agenda

Considerations involved in deciding where to place an issue on the agenda may include the desire to create an optimistic atmosphere, likely alertness or fatigue of the participants, and signaling the importance of an issue.

(B) Increasing the number of issues or dividing the existing issues into more manageable parts ("fractionating")

In some instances increasing the number of issues allows for greater flexibility in the "give and take," in the sense that there can be concessions gained or given on different issues. This is in contrast to single-issue situations, in which all the bargaining is centered on the one item. This last circumstance becomes particularly difficult if it develops into a winner-takes-all battle. There are, though, some potential disadvantages in adding issues, including greater complexity, increasing the length of the negotiations, linking issues in an undesirable fashion, and being open to the charge of belatedly raising new points.

(C) Issue control[5]

Less generalized issues are frequently easier to manage than those that are magnified in terms of scope and consequences. Hence one can sometimes "control the issue" by limiting its significance through "localizing" its impact and making it more time, place, and outcome specific. For example, if one argues that the settlement of a given issue will be precedent setting for an indefinite period, the solution is likely to be approached cautiously and with considerable concern. This may, in fact, block a reasonable agreement that would have been possible if the likely consequences had not been so magnified. Hence particularizing an issue and treating the matter as a one-off situation is sometimes useful.

(D) Issue rigidity

This refers to the presentation of an issue in such a manner that there is little room for maneuvering or mutual concessions. Obviously, this type of issue formulation runs the risk of engendering stern opposition and increases the possibility of no agreement being reached.

(E) Central issues[6]

There is more likelihood of difficulty in the negotiations if both parties consider the same issue to be of greatest importance to them. Sometimes it is desirable to add issues so as to try to lessen the intensive concentration on the one item. By so doing it may demonstrate that the participants' key concerns differ. This tends to allow for more flexibility in the negotiations.

(F) Disposing of selected issues

As the negotiation on issues develops, it may be feasible, as well as good tactics, for the participants to withdraw those issues that are not essential and that, potentially, represent a high cost threat to the adversary. This tactic may best be pursued on a mutual concession basis and it could occur well into the negotiating process, not just when the issues are being originally defined.[7]

It is important to be sensitive to the fact that in addition to the explicit and tangible issues about which the negotiations are centered other intangible concerns, such as honor, reputation, image, and face may also play a very significant role in the process. These intangibles may be present from the start or may emerge as a result of the dynamics of the process. It is such "hidden" issues that often explain apparent self-defeating or irrational behavior in reaching agreement on explicit items.

Action Guide!

Since it is difficult to confront intangible issues head on, it is desirable, whenever possible, to convert them into more manageable and tangible ones. For example, you can "allow" an opponent success on a concrete item of noncrucial significance, permitting your adversary to have a sense of increased self-esteem.

Although agenda construction and the identification and ordering of issues are usually more systematic and formalized in symmetrical representational negotiation (and third-party negotiations), they do occur in asymmetrical and one-on-one transactions. For instance, a human service worker, preparing for a negotiating interview with a nonvoluntary antagonistic client (asymmetrical-representational), may well plan out ahead of time an agenda for their meeting. This planning is likely to involve decisions as to which issues should be discussed and in what order. Of course, the client's agenda (overt or covert) might be quite different from that of the worker; hence these differences might have to be negotiated.

Another example is two workers (one-on-one) who meet to negotiate their personal/professional dispute over "territorial imperatives" (types of cases). Prior to their conference, each may have made a mental list of the issues to be put forward. But once the meeting begins they may find they have to negotiate in order to arrive at a mutually acceptable written or unwritten agenda.

Don't overlook the fact that the process of gaining acceptance of one's own definition of the situation (including issues) is itself a key part of the negotiating process. And the "greater a party's relative power, the greater the likelihood that its definition of bargaining issue will prevail" (Bacharach & Lawler, 1981, pp. 166-167).

The following Action Guide is consistent with our discussion of agenda-building.

Action Guide!

In constructing the agenda, start with topics that are likely to create goodwill, cooperativeness, and optimism. It is often useful to start with an item that is relatively simple and tangible. Such an issue offers a good possibility for a mutually satisfactory outcome, even if of limited significance. An early success of this sort tends to build confidence and generate a positive momentum.

PHASE 2. OPENING MOVES: ADVANCING
DEMANDS AND UNCOVERING INTERESTS

After establishing the agenda, the opening moves in negotiations usually consist of each side putting forth its positions or demands. This gambit is particularly characteristic of the distributive strategy, although it may also be used as part of an integrative approach.

Assuming the distributive strategy, what guidelines should be kept in mind? Typically, the opening bid in the bargaining process should be relatively high. There are four good reasons for this: It helps to set the "bargaining range"; it avoids the danger of conceding too much initially, through a miscalculation of the other party's real expectations; it allows room for later concessions; and, finally, it demonstrates determination, both to your opponents and to your constituents. However, certain cautions should be kept in mind in respect to high initial bids. If the bids are excessively high they may discourage further negotiations or create an impression of incompetence, inexperience, or irresponsibility. In addition, they may backfire by generating unrealistic expectations on the part of the constituents, thus making later concessions more difficult, with the added danger of a "disillusioned" constituency withdrawing support from its negotiator.

A less typical early move, but one favored by those using an integrative strategy, is to focus on uncovering the interests of the negotiating parties. Since this tactic is not as well known as more conventional maneuvers, and because it offers promising possibilities, we will elaborate on it.

Fisher and Ury (1981, chaps. 1, 3) are leading proponents of a variation of the integrative approach. They refer to their version as "principled negotiation" (or "negotiating on the merits"). An important tactical component of their strategy is focusing on interests, rather than on positions or demands.

The basic assumptions underlying the argument that negotiations should center on reconciling interests, rather than positions, are (a) that a variety of possible positions might satisfy any given interest, allowing for more flexibility and choices, and (b) that *shared* as well as conflicting interests usually lie behind opposing positions. Following from these assumptions is the *suggested tactic of trying, early on in the process, to identify the interests of your opponent, as well as of being clear and effective in presenting your own interests.* The purpose of negotiating is to serve your interests while searching/inventing options that will provide mutual benefits as well. It is a further premise of this approach that the most powerful interests reside in basic human needs.

The Action Guide that follows offers suggestion as to how to implement the above tactic.

Action Guide!

To discover your opponents' interests, put yourself "in their shoes" and try to figure out why they take certain positions while rejecting others. You might even wish to make a written list, as the ideas come to you, of the interests of the various parties and the importance that they appear to have in their hierarchies of desires.

Remember, despite its emphasis on flexibility, the "interest" strategy is not soft. It accepts the need for firmness in negotiations.

The principled negotiating approach, with its focus on interests, has important advantages and should be in the forefront of the consciousness of any negotiator. It represents a very real advance over many of the traditional ideas about negotiation. Nevertheless, we suggest that it is not a panacea and is neither appropriate nor effective in all situations. Some of the adherents of this approach appear to be caught up in an unduly uncritical enthusiasm for it.

In our judgment, the "interest *rather* than position" approach tends to (a) exaggerate the differences between a flexible positional approach and an interest orientation, (b) underestimate the role of power resources, (c) afford insufficient recognition to the possibility of truly incompatible key interests, (d) make a somewhat presumptuous claim to being the "principled" approach, (e) demonstrate a rationalistic bias, and (f) treat the negotiation process as an enclave without putting it within the broader context. Too little attention is paid to the difficulty of getting negotiations started and to the political/social and value settings of the negotiating process. We believe, as previously stated, that no single approach is effective in all situations and that actual negotiations frequently require a calculated mixture of the positional and interests substrategies.

PHASE 3. INTENSIFICATION OF THE
NEGOTIATIONS: BARGAINING AND
DISCOVERING NEW OPTIONS

Differences tend to be accentuated during the beginning period of this phase. Flowing from the articulation of divergent positions or interests is a "heating up" of the negotiating process. And if the distributive mode of negotiating predominates, the bargaining may get especially tough, with a sharp edge to the give and take. This is when promises, threats, bluffing, and "dirty tricks," or even personal attacks, are most likely to emerge.

During this stage those employing the integrative strategy are likely to seek greater specification of the interests and issues, identify the desired outcomes, and seek out the "merits" of the requirements and objectives that have been advanced. As the phase progresses, if all goes well, realistic possibilities are discussed and compromises emerge or new options are "invented." Thus differences are narrowed and the basis for agreement begins to develop.

At this point, a more detailed examination of the dynamics of work during the intensive phase of negotiation will be useful. For clarity's sake we will discuss the processes within the two strategic options separately, starting with the distributive. As Chart 7.1 indicates, this is the place in the distributive approach when debate and bargaining come to the fore.

The Dynamics of the Distributive Option
During the Intensive Phase

(1) *Debate:* An essential feature of negotiations is persuasion through debate. In our usage debate includes argumentation, that is, the marshaling of facts and the presentation of a series of steps based on logical reasoning. It also involves generating understanding, correcting stereotypes, and promoting relearning.

The techniques of gentle persuasion were discussed in an earlier chapter. Although many of the same mechanisms are involved in debate within the framework of negotiations, two differences should be highlighted. The first is that debate, as part of the give-and-take process, is frequently more "hard sell" than "gentle persuasion." Second, debate within negotiations using the distributive approach is frequently intermixed with bargaining and its associated techniques. Hence, the character of the debate is influenced by its interplay with other tactics and by the general strategy of distributive negotiation, of which it is an important tactic.

(2) *Bargaining:* Two basic dilemmas confronting bargainers are, first, how to offer cooperative cues (e.g., a willingness to give some concessions and to be reasonable) without such actions being seen by the other party as indicators of weakness and an invitation to exploitation, and second, how and when to use pressure tactics in such a way that they won't produce a counterproductive escalation (e.g., counterthreats).

The bargaining process can be construed as a mixture of inducements (carrots) and sanctions (sticks). Inducements consist of provisional offers and counteroffers—tactical concessions—that reduce the difference between bargainers on an issue, while sanctions are grounded in punitive capabilities that permit bargainers to threaten and damage each other. (Bacharach & Lawler, 1981, p. 104)

Keep in mind that while bargaining is most characteristic of the distributive strategy, it appears, however tempered, in most forms of negotiation.

(a) "Carrots" and "Sticks"

Carrots and sticks, such as promises and threats, play a very important part in the bargaining tactic. It is not surprising that promises are more likely to be considered legitimate than are threats. There are some situations in which threats may be seen as acceptable, though not desirable (e.g., when used defensively).[8] Obviously, promises and other reward offers tend not to be as potentially destructive to the negotiating process as are coercive threats. However, even promises, such as those that are empty or extravagant, may be seen as inappropriate, or even designed to "corrupt." In such instances, promises are counterproductive.

The effects of promises or threats appear to be significantly influenced by such considerations as the ability to make good on the promise or threat, on the magnitude and potential impact of the "carrot or stick," and on the immediacy of the probable consequence. More immediate consequences are likely to have a greater effect. The manner of presentation may be of decisive significance. Also, promises or threats are likely to be more effective if the recipients know precisely how they are supposed to respond to them. In other words, what are the expected behavioral changes?

Another point worth keeping in mind is that the most effective promise or threat is not always that directed toward the negotiators themselves. For instance, in a hostage situation the threat to a third party (the hostage) may have more impact than threats aimed directly at the negotiators.

Although research on the effects of promises and threats is not definitive, it does suggest that promises and threats should be used only when other means of influence aren't available or do not appear to be effective.[9]

Threats and punitive tactics are clearly dangerous "weapons." They may result in conflict escalation, retaliation, lessened willingness to make concessions over the long haul, a breaking off of negotiations, and the destruction of personal relationships. The use of coercive power has the ever-present potential of invoking "open resistance and anger from the strong and often inauthentic cooperation and resentment from the weak" (Deutsch, 1977, p. 142). Yet, it would be an error to write off such means as being totally self-defeating, or inappropriate, in negotiations. In given situations it may be necessary to use coercion. For instance, on occasion adversaries will not negotiate in good faith, or on the basis of reasonableness, unless the potential costs to them are made very explicit and alarming. And in given circumstances threats do tend to increase the likelihood of concession-making by the other party.

In order to use coercion effectively in bargaining, and with as little risk as possible, it is important that the person using such means be perceived by the other party as acting defensively, and without aggressive motivation. These conditions tend to exist when the coercive action is perceived as not intended to punish or be used for selfish purposes, and is supported by acceptable norms concerning self-protection. Conciliatory, face-saving, and regret-type gestures also tend to lessen the likelihood of generating countercoercive measures.[10]

Four factors that contribute to the credibility of threats are the real or "assumed" personality of the person making the threat (e.g., "touchy" people who are quick to anger and are perceived as likely to carry out threats rising out of frustration); the actor's freedom from control by reasonable third parties; the threatener's "fate control" over the recipient and the latter's lack of retaliatory capacity; and the perceived tenuousness of the "hold" of restraining norms on the person making the threat.

Despite the limitations and cautions in respect to threats and coercive means, we agree with Bacharach and Lawler (1981, p. 109) that punitive tactics are an integral part of bargaining. But remember, because of the risks (e.g., retaliation, escalation), the use of coercion in bargaining should be considered a measure of last resort.

What should be done if one is on the receiving end of coercive threats? The suggestions in the following Action Guide might prove useful.

Action Guide!

When Threatened, Don't Panic! Try These Countercoercion Measures

— Refuse to "accept" the threat or give the impression that it was not "heard" or interpreted as a threat.

— Build up your retaliatory capacities and strengthen the impression that they will be used in appropriate circumstances.

— Get assistance or protection from a third party, or join in an alliance in order to strengthen joint retaliatory capabilities.

— Demonstrate less "need" for whatever had been sought from the threatener, thus reducing dependency on that party. This might involve raising the possibility of dealing with another "supplier" of the desired items or services.

— Generate guilt and concern on the part of the threatener by invoking moral commitments, indicating "hurt" or a sense of betrayal.

— Reduce, or deflect, the aggression of the person making threats by persuading the threatener that the responsibility for the circumstances or frustration leading to the threat does not really rest with you.[11]

(b) Bluffing

Bluffing represents another aspect of the give and take of bargaining. It is most commonly employed as a deliberate effort to create a mildly distorted or a strongly illusionary impression as to the power relationship between the contending parties.[12] An *offensive* bluff is one directed toward portraying the opponent's position as being more vulnerable than it really is, while a *defensive* bluff is used to give an inflated picture of one's own resources and/or willingness to use them.

Obviously, bluffing can be a risky activity. The infrequent bluff that is coupled with actual strength is likely to be much more effective, and contain many fewer risks, than bluffing that is overused and not backed up by significant resources. Bluffing may prove most useful in short-term bargaining relationships that are unlikely to recur and in which long-term credibility is not a significant consideration.

There is a distinction (even if not always clear-cut) between bluffing and outright lying, or gross misrepresentation. Bluffing is not usually considered to be a "dirty trick," but deliberate falsification is considered outside the pale of "ethical" negotiations. One characteristic of bluffing that should be kept in mind is that it has a tendency to get out of hand—that is, to be used excessively and inappropriately. Such a misuse can be very damaging. Clearly, the decision as to whether or not to engage in bluffing requires a careful assessment of the potential benefits/cost and of one's skill in employing it.

(c) Give and Take

The exchange of concessions is a critical part of the give-and-take process. It is at the heart of the bargaining tactic—a vital part of negotiations, particularly when the distributive approach is employed.

"Concessional exchange" is a complex process involving a range of modes of influence, including many to which we've already referred (e.g., promises/threats, persuasion, etc.). Although there is much theorizing about how "exchanging" occurs in the bargaining situation, there is considerably less empirical data than might be inferred from some of the writings on the subject.

With this overall disclaimer in mind, the following cautious generalizations are offered.

(1) Concessions are not necessarily made along one dimension or in accordance with a simple standard of equivalence. Rather, they are "matched" in a complex and sometimes hard-to-define manner. For instance, consider the difficulty of equating work in a hazardous environment with a higher salary. How much is a risk to one's health worth in monetary terms? What is a fair exchange?

(2) A plausible general statement about the dynamics of the exchange of concessions is that one's anticipation of one's adversary's behavior in regard to concessions is likely to influence one's own actions.[13] For instance, this suggests that one's probable response to the anticipation that an opponent may make a large concession rather readily is to take a tougher stand on the granting of concessions. Another response to the same anticipation, though, could be gentler behavior. It is also likely that concessions will be made most readily by the participant with the greater eagerness, or necessity, to reach an agreement.

It is clearly advantageous for bargainers to give the impression that their assessment of the risk to them is low and/or their willingness to accept it is high. This stance suggests that they are not likely to make concessions easily, nor that such concessions will be of great magnitude. There is evidence to support the contention that "tougher concession tactics result in more concessions than softer ones" (Bacharach & Lawler, 1981, p. 83). However, it has also been observed that if this tough posture is a bluff it may prove costly in the long run. This is because larger concessions than would have been the case at an earlier point might eventually have to be made if the bluff is called.

(3) The willingness to make a concession can signal various things. It isn't necessarily a sign of weakness. For instance, it may simply suggest a realistic appraisal of the situation, or it may indicate that the time for serious bargaining has arrived. Or it may be used to "test" the opponent's goodwill. It may even involve offering a seemingly significant concession for one in return when, in fact, that which is granted is of little real importance to the maker of the concession.

(4) The most common behavior in bargaining is a coming together of concessions: "That convergence may come through a gradual inching toward agreement—or through substantial concessions to or near the final outcome" (Gulliver, 1979, p. 164).

Specific concessional techniques have been identified in the literature. One of these is to start with a competitive approach, then to follow it up with a cooperative gesture. There is some experimental evidence that a cooperative bid is more likely to elicit a positive response from the other party when it is advanced within the context of some noncooperative moves. In other words, if you are always cooperative yet another positive gesture might have limited impact; this is a type of "marginal utility" in cooperative offers.

A second technique involves providing "compensation" for the loss experienced by your adversary in making a concession, that is, giving something else that is desired. Such compensatory benefits may be in the same realm as the loss, or they may serve different needs, or be in a different "currency." Of course, as we have already pointed out, it is often difficult to determine equivalency in this type of substitutive compensation (e.g., more money for loss of status). The process of establishing substitutability may be made easier if a reasonable rationale for linking the concession and compensation can be identified, thus providing a basis for rationalizing the granting of a given concession and accepting a substitute. For example, if a husband and wife make an agreement that one will do the washing and the other the shopping, each activity may be linked by being time-consuming and not desired, but necessary for the household.

A third technique that might be useful under some circumstances is that of "graduated reciprocity." What this requires is a *unilateral* cooperative act (i.e., only one of the adversaries makes a concession) which is clearly identified ahead of time as being designed to reduce tension and bring about an agreement. The opponent is then invited to reciprocate. If the opponent reacts positively (this may be only after several concessional acts), a reward of an appropriate extent and type should be offered.[14]

This technique requires a very careful assessment of the potential risk. And it is extremely important, while making such moves, not to let one's capacity to retaliate deteriorate, or be undermined. It should be kept in mind that unilateral cooperative acts (concessions) run the danger of being misinterpreted as indicators of weakness, thus generating the risk of inviting exploitation.

A fourth technique is to use a cluster of devices designed to reinforce the impression that you will "hang tough." Such actions might include contending that you are under binding instructions from your constituency, or that your constituency will be difficult to restrain; imposing time pressures on the other party in regard to a given concession or an overall agreement; and conveying the impression that you are a battle-hardened, and not unduly squeamish, veteran of equally or even more intense conflicts.

Value arguments also play a part in the bargaining process, including the giving and receiving of concessions. Three basic value stances are employed in distributive bargaining. The first is the claim for equal benefits in regard to payoffs or concessions. This "equality" approach is usually based on some concept of justice. A second value argument is that of "equity," that is, there should be a correspondence between what one gives or contributes and what one receives (e.g., if you contribute more you should get more). Included in the equity notion may be the premise that the benefit should reflect the inequality in the power of the contenders. Finally, there is the "responsibility" argument. This value position attaches primary importance to meeting the legitimate requirements or needs of others, even if the benefits are unequally distributed in favor of the party that is more vulnerable or who contributes less.

Bacharach and Lawler (1981, p. 176) have advanced several propositions that link power, interests, and value arguments:

Proposition 1. The greater the difference in bargaining power, the greater the tendency of the higher-power party to use equity appeals and the greater the tendency of the lower-power party to use equality or responsibility appeals.

Proposition 2. If the difference in bargaining power is very large, the lower-power party will tend to use responsibility appeals; if the power difference is not large, the lower-power party will tend to use equality appeals.

Proposition 3. If the bargaining power of both parties is very high, they are likely to use equality appeals.

Experienced negotiators will find that the above propositions are easy to relate to. They are of particular importance in making clear that value arguments are not devoid of power and interest components. For instance, a claim for social justice on the basis of the responsibility norm is an important weapon in the tactical approach of low-power groups. This may be supported by an implied threat of discontent on the part of a deprived constituency if basic needs are not met. In turn, the claim, however masked, that "might is right" in terms of an advantageous outcome (equity norm) for one of the participants is frequently advanced by powerful persons or groups. However, it also needs to be recognized that generalizations, such as the above propositions, are "tendencies" and that the actors in bargaining dramas don't always follow the script. For example, socially conscious, powerful persons may, in some cases, respond positively to humanitarian (responsibility) values. Nevertheless, the basic "truth" of the linkage among value arguments, power, and interests should be kept in mind by those in bargaining situations.

The above discussion of value arguments ought to raise a cautionary flag in the mind of a negotiator. It suggests that claims of "principle" should be carefully assessed. Principles can be misused, and people can hold "destructive" principles. Or an inappropriate personal rigidity may be confused with principled behavior. Note, too, that some people in conflict situations tend to follow a pattern of saying, "In principle, I agree with your position *but*. . . ." After hearing this said on numerous occasions, one might be justified in wondering what this claimed adherence to a principle really amounts to.

Some people are quite adroit in using principles in conflictual situations as a basis for unprincipled behavior. I recall one situation (in a climate of political fear) when the rationalizing of inactivity against repressive legislation was justified, by understandably frightened people, on the basis of a variety of suddenly discovered or invented principles. A colleague who could no longer stand the painful rationalizations and hypocrisy arose in a meeting and, in a ringing voice, proclaimed: "Ladies and Gentlemen, it is clear that now is the time to rise above principles." The point was made—all too clearly for some.

The list of possible techniques in regard to the give and take of bargaining is almost unlimited.[15] They range from emphasizing that the other party should have "to work" for every concession gained, to remembering the importance of "no-cost" rewarding of your opponent (e.g., showing respect), and to avoiding "dumb mistakes," such as accepting your opponent's first offer.[16] There is one suggested technique that is particularly colorful in its formulation (it is said to be based on a Chinese saying). It is to "resist like water." The notion here is that negotiators, like water confronting pressure, should fall back; then, when it suits them, they should seep and creep back, at first slowly and then more strongly.

The Dynamics of the Integrative Option
During the Intensive Phase

In the earlier phase of this option the emphasis in the negotiations was on identifying, understanding, and communicating interests. This included trying to get behind positions to the underlying interests. To make sure the understandings were correct and the perceptions accurate, the participants might have been invited to summarize their own and their opponents' interests in a positive manner. This assists in the process of locating commonalities and differences in the interests of the participants.

(1) *Further interest exploration and the use of objective criteria.* The use of objective criteria means emphasizing the standard of fairness, examining data and possible outcomes, and considering possible solutions in terms of the merits of the arguments.[17] According to those prominent proponents of this approach, Fisher and Ury, negotiating on merit has three main elements: dealing with each issue as a shared search for fair and objective criteria, being reasonable and accessible to reasoned argument as to appropriate standards and their application, and acting on the basis of principle and merit rather than yielding to pressure. Flexibility as well as firmness are also key words in this approach.

In the intense discussion that characterizes this phase of negotiations, attempts are made to find solutions by reconciling interests (rather than positions, which is what is emphasized in the distributive approach). During these negotiations areas of agreement and disagreement are reexamined and issues reformulated. In practice, a form of debate and bargaining goes on, hence there is an overlap here between the two strategic options.

(2) *"Inventing" new options: The discovery of mutually beneficial solutions.* A vital aspect of the integrative approach is the discovery of solutions that provide significant mutual gains for both parties. These mutual gain options may be thought of as "superordinate solutions." They include, but go beyond, the prior definitions of interests and issues. These new solutions provide a possible basis for agreement.

Considerable creativity is involved in formulating these superordinate options. Hence the advocates of the integrative strategic approach pay a good deal of attention to techniques for "inventing" options. One of the most detailed discussions of such techniques is that found in Fisher and Ury (1981, pp. 62, 68-73). They present a prescription for generating new options. It consists of the following:

— Separate the act of inventing options from the act of judging them.
— Broaden the options on the table rather than look for a single answer.
— Search for mutual gains.
— Invent ways of making their (the other parties') decisions easy.

The major technique used is "brainstorming." In this process the generated ideas should not be evaluated, or decided upon, in the initial stage. Steps fundamental to the enterprise of inventing options are focussing on a specific problem, diagnosing the particular issue in general terms, considering what ought to be done, and, finally, emerging with some specific ideas for action based upon the prior steps.

Pruitt and Lewis (1977, p. 157) put the integrative approach—with its emphasis on inventing options and bridging different interests and demands—in what we consider to be a realistic perspective when they write:

> Totally integrative agreements, in which both parties get all they were seeking, occasionally occur as the result of the discovery of a bridging formula, but such agreements are quite rare. It is usually necessary for one or both parties to make selective concessions, in search of a partially integrative alternative.

This statement highlights our contention that concessional bargaining and the discovery of new, superordinate options are not totally discrete activities: They are frequently entwined.

PHASE 4. WORKING OUT AN AGREEMENT

Although there are also differences between the distributive and integrative options, in this phase the overlap is sufficient so that we shall consider them together.

The latter phase of a negotiating session may well be the most critical time since there is a tendency for agreements to be reached at, or near, the deadline. Factors that contribute to an agreement being arrived at include recognition that the point in negotiations that has been reached offers a reasonably satisfactory result; belief that the other party has reached the end of making concessions and that the differences have been narrowed as much as they are likely to be; external pressure to arrive at a settlement; sheer exhaustion; and the emergence of what Pruitt and Lewis (1977, p. 69) refer to as a "mutually prominent alternative." Such an alternative usually develops over a period of time (although it may have been there at the start of the process). It is a conclusion that both parties sense as the very likely or inevitable outcome of the negotiations. This type of perceived outcome may be the result of complex bargaining over different preferential alternatives, or it may be the consequence of the invention of a new mutual benefit option (as stressed in the integrative approach).

There are some additional tactics and techniques that might be considered if the usual methods of reaching a final agreement prove inadequate or insufficient by themselves. One is to settle for an agreement on some of the points, rather than to try for an overall "solution." A reverse variant of this is to "threaten" to reconsider the items already agreed to if a final inclusive agreement is not reached. And a sometimes useful, coaxing technique is to stress the point that "it would be a shame, since we have come this far and overcome so many difficulties, if we weren't able to reach a final agreement." This type of statement can be reinforced either by implying that it would be "letting the side down" if a positive outcome wasn't achieved, or by the "reluctant threat" that others (e.g., the public) might react quite negatively if no resolution was forthcoming.

One additional mechanism to consider if there is resistance to finalizing an agreement because of uncertainty as to how it will work out in practice is the *reopener* provision. This is an agreement that after a given period of time the decision arrived at by the parties will be subject to reexamination and possible modification. There are two main versions of this approach: One is that some or all aspects of the agreement that was concluded may be reconsidered after a specific time, without any strings attached; the other is that if the agreed-on criteria for judging the effectiveness of the joint decision are not met by the time a reexamination is called for, then the alternative proposal advanced by the "loser" will be adopted.

There are both pros and cons in regard to reopener provisions. A strong positive consideration is that it may make a satisfactory agreement possible, thus preventing a deadlock or a less desirable resolution. However, there are also some potentially negative consequences that should be kept in mind. These include a lowered incentive to make the original agreement a success, and increased tension between the parties due to a lack of confidence as to the other party's commitment to the original agreement. Pruitt and Lewis (1977, p. 161) make the following points regarding the circumstances that appear to be congruent with a "reopener" provision:

(A) If the future conditions are quite uncertain and there is genuine question as to how the original agreement will work in practice, then a reopener provision might make sense.

(B) If the risks associated with the signed agreement are very considerable, and if there are serious potential costs for one or both parties associated with the possible failure of the agreement to work out in practice, then a reopener proviso might be desirable.

However, these considerations should be balanced against the potentially negative results of a reopener arrangement.

An experienced negotiator will recognize that in many cases a bad agreement is worse than a deadlock; thus peace at any price is to be avoided. There is also evidence that "turning the other cheek" is often an invitation to exploitation, rather than being the route to constructive cooperation. Two approaches to deciding whether or not to reach an agreement are the "bottom line" position and "BATNA" (best alternative to a negotiated agreement).[18] *Bottom line* refers to the poorest outcome that one will accept in an agreement. Since the bottom line is usually determined ahead of time, it may be very useful in preventing the negotiator from falling victim to immediate temptations, panic, or pressure. On the other hand, it may limit the negotiator's ability to respond to new situations arising out of the very process of the negotiation. I found the bottom line approach useful, for example, in bargaining for an Oriental carpet in a community in which such negotiations were the norm. However, the danger of rigidity in such an approach is a real one.

The BATNA guideline has some real advantages. It leads one to ask, what is the best alternative available if I don't accept the proposed agreement? This approach forces the negotiator to think systematically, but flexibly, about what the consequences will be if no agreement is reached. It provides a different kind of baseline, one that allows the ongoing experiences of the negotiating process to enter into the calculations rather than relying on a "cut-off" point determined prior to the negotiations. As Fisher and Ury (1981, pp. 104-105) correctly argue, "If you have not thought carefully about what you will do if you fail to reach an agreement, you are negotiating with your eyes closed." They add the further interesting caution that "in most circumstances the greatest danger is that you are too committed to reaching agreement."

In the final stages of agreement making it is also very important to ensure that steps for implementation and follow-up are decided upon and that a "monitoring" mechanism is in place. Remember, too, the importance of the "ritual affirmation" at the time the final agreement is executed. Even though it may be a bit painful after a heated bargaining session to appear cordial and shake hands or share a drink with your adversary, the benefits of such a "gracious" gesture may far outweigh the costs, allowing for smoother future transactions. And, finally, don't claim victory, appear smug, or exude triumph!

At the beginning of this chapter, we indicated that although our emphasis would be on representational negotiation of the symmetrical type, much of what was discussed would be relevant to the other interactional forms as well. In the next section we will amplify this point, as well as highlight some variations in negotiations associated with the different interactional types.

ASYMMETRICAL AND ONE-ON-ONE NEGOTIATIONS

Most of the previous discussion in this chapter, which was based on the symmetrical/representational model, applies as well to asymmetrical and one-on-one negotiatory transactions. For instance, in negotiating with a client of an agency (asymmetrical representational) or a colleague (one-on-one), building trust, effective communications, decoupling the person from the issue, achieving one's definition of the situation, bargaining, and creating new options are all of great potential importance. Thus the strategic considerations, tactics, techniques, and processes already discussed have across-the-board relevance.

Even though there are many commonalities, there are certain differences related to the type of interaction. It is to these variations that we now turn. Keep in mind that these differences often tend to be matters of degree, rather than kind. Conflicts between colleagues are frequently unexpected and diffuse. This is true to a lesser extent in worker-client interactions. In the case of such "spontaneous" conflicts there isn't the opportunity to plan ahead in respect to the agenda or strategies and tactics. This suggests that the handling of many one-on-one conflicts is necessarily nonsystematic. Also, less tangible issues, including those of face and esteem, frequently occupy a more significant place in these types of conflict transactions.

Another characteristic attribute of many one-on-one and asymmetrical interactions is the combining of different kinds of conflicts. For instance, conflicts of interest/belief may get thoroughly mixed with expressive, displaced, illusionary, or misattributed types. Hence different tactics (e.g., opportunity for ventilation) may be required. An example of this interweaving of conflict types is when two colleagues who work together closely don't like each other, as well as having substantially different interests. Hence the problem of sorting out the conflict sources and types in such a situation may be particularly important, as well as complex.

Personal characteristics are likely to play an important part in these types of conflicts. The fact that there is less control by external structures and groups allows the social-psychological attributes of the participants to have more opportunity for expression and impact. This goes hand in hand with the greater likelihood of heightened emotions in these encounters. The content of one-on-one disputes may also sometimes differ from that commonly found in representational (symmetrical) transactions. For instance, conflicts over "identities" and informal role definitions are not uncommon in one-on-one interactions between workers in an agency.

As suggested, differences in the nature of representational (symmetrical) and one-on-one conflict situations may well influence the choice of tactics and techniques. For one thing, the modes of conflict management are more likely to be blurred. Thus negotiation and the use of unexpressed or clandestine means (e.g., covert resistance or manipulation) may become inextricably meshed. Also, the various strategies, and their accompanying tactics, may be not only less formalized but also used in an implicit rather than explicit manner. For instance, two workers who have different religious values and attitudes may develop a tacit understanding (agreement) through implicit negotiations to avoid certain "sensitive" subjects (e.g., abortion).

Another example of the use of implicit give and take would be when the tension that developed between two workers, both of whom had romantic intentions toward a third, was resolved through tacit negotiations that resulted in one of the competitors "backing off." In this type of implicit conflict management, nonverbal signals may be particularly important. Furthermore, making implicit negotiations explicit may have an adverse effect. This latter point is related to the fact that in many forms of social exchange it is "outside the pale" to articulate the expected reciprocal action. For instance, when you invite a person to dinner you may do so with the *implicit* understanding that you would be receptive to a reciprocal invitation. However, think of the likely reaction that would be invoked if you sent a written invitation to a person to come to dinner at your home with a "P.S." indicating that you expect a return invitation.

There is one caution regarding worker-client conflicts that requires reiteration—the danger in the tendency by some workers to use a helping approach when the appropriate strategy is negotiation or authoritative decision making. The differences between the conflict management and helping functions were explored in an earlier chapter. And this distinction will be highlighted again in the following discussion on the human service worker and the nonvoluntary client.

THE HUMAN SERVICE WORKER
AND THE NONVOLUNTARY CLIENT

Although there are many times in working with *voluntary* clients that negotiation is employed (e.g., developing a mutually acceptable contract), this strategy is usually even more prominent in the context of worker-nonvoluntary client relationships. In our usage, the concept of "nonvoluntary" extends from the client who is simply indifferent to the required transaction with the worker to the person who actively objects to it, often with considerable antagonism.

Nonvoluntary clients usually become involved with human service workers due to legal requirements, or because of pressure from friends, neighbors, significant others, police, or social agencies. Examples of such clients might be child or spouse abusers, probationers or parolees, beneficiaries (potential or actual) of various assistance programs, and even, in some circumstances, persons who hope to become adopting parents.

The worker-nonvoluntary client transaction may be characterized by opposing interests, differing definitions of the situation, and conflicting loyalties and commitments.[19] Hence the relationship between the worker and client may be one of conflict, rather than of conforming to the cooperative and shared goals "model" on which much of the practice with voluntary clients is based. For this reason the parties in such transactions may be viewed as contenders in a conflict situation, a perspective that is quite different from that which usually characterizes the traditional "helping" situation. "Nonvoluntary situations often require that attention be directed primarily not to healing but to negotiating strategies" (Murdach, 1980, pp. 458-459).

What often exists in such an interaction is a strong social control element, with the human service worker employing socially authorized power/influence in the context of a conflict of interests between the client and some aspect of the social environment. Since the agency represents some part of that environment, the worker, in speaking for the organization, is involved in a representational transaction. It is ordinarily asymmetrical because the client in these circumstances does not usually have a constituency. Although the worker and client may be contenders, with different interests, it is important for the worker to convey the sense that "an adversary is not necessarily the same as an enemy" (Cingolani, 1984, p. 445).

The tactics and techniques used in the negotiations between workers and nonvoluntary clients are essentially those already discussed. Bargaining and debate are essential aspects of this type of transaction. However, in some of these situations the workers may also have to use their authority to insist on compliance by clients, despite the latters' opposition. Whenever feasible and appropriate, though, it is preferable to negotiate, rather than enforce. Also, it is important for workers to avoid taking a "false" role, such as a mediator, when in fact they are representative of one of the interests involved.

As we have already stressed, the primary strategies, tactics, and techniques employed in the conflict management aspects of working with nonvoluntary clients are similar to those used in the other transactional categories. Although traditional helping activities and techniques play a part in transactions with some nonvoluntary clients, it is clear that a conflict management "model" is often of major importance in such interactions. The particular balance of the two approaches will vary, of course, with the specific situation.

ROLE CONFLICT NEGOTIATION

Negotiations in respect to role conflicts are typically conducted on a one-on-one or asymmetrical basis. The latter frequently involves a subordinate-superordinate transaction. Although there are various ways of *unilaterally* coping with role conflicts (e.g., leaving a position, abridging the role network, evading observation), bilateral efforts to manage such conflicts often have more positive consequences (Feld & Radin, 1982, pp. 94-96). Such bilateral transactions may involve negotiations centering on revising or compromising role expectations, or modifying patterns of interaction and communication. For instance, should a private secretary be expected to make coffee for the employer? This particular question of role expectations may develop special overtones and conflictual elements if the employer is male and the secretary female. Another example of role conflict would be a situation in which a worker and a member of the board of management of a home for the aged differ as to which one should make the final decision concerning the eligibility of a person for scarce accommodation. In both of the above, examples of the potential or actual role conflicts might be managed through negotiations.

DIRTY TRICKS

The use of dirty tricks in negotiations, whether representational or one-on-one, symmetrical or asymmetrical, is by no means unknown. Even "principled" negotiators sometimes cannot resist the temptation to win by any means. The use of such devices is most likely when the stakes are high or there is strong antagonism between the adversaries. The following brief discussion of dirty tricks is not intended to provide the reader with the wherewithal or cover of legitimacy to employ such means. Rather, it is intended to be useful in a defensive manner, that is, to assist in countering such activities.

By dirty tricks we mean such tactics and techniques as deliberate lying and misrepresentation, unethical coercion, deception, unfair disadvantaging (e.g., environmental manipulation), and the intentional generating of stress. Our ethical stance in regard to responding to such tactics/techniques was discussed in a prior chapter. Essentially, the position taken is that defensive retaliation in like manner is justifiable under certain *limited* circumstances. However, in terms of both effectiveness and matters of principle it is greatly preferable to use less undesirable means to counter dirty tricks.

One general recommendation is not to trust an opponent unless you have good reason to do so. This implies that it is desirable in negotiations to rely on objective verification as much as possible. In this way, you make yourself less vulnerable to dirty tricks (Fisher & Ury, 1981, pp. 135-136, 138). It is sometimes useful when dirty tricks are being used, to bring them out into the open and question their use. However, it is desirable to challenge the means rather than the person. Also, it should be made clear to the other party that you will not continue the negotiations unless there can be agreement about the "rules of the game." Often, the very fact that your adversary knows that you are not naive and a "sitting duck" will improve matters, that is, if the other party genuinely wants to negotiate. If the negotiating process is really a facade then it is probably best for this to become clear.

An overall guideline is that a contender should neither accept being treated badly nor allow a commitment to being a well-mannered and "nice" person to make oneself vulnerable to exploitation. There is a reverse risk as well: Some people are too quick to assume they are being "done in" and confuse hard but ethical bargaining with unethical behavior. This reaction can be self-defeating as far as successful negotiations are concerned. The more general use of dirty tricks (not just in negotiations) has been explored, in more detail, in the prior discussion of "Managing Conflict by Covert Means."

Some final suggestions in regard to negotiation, and to the broader conflict management process, are advanced in the following Action Guide.

Action Guide!

Don't approach negotiations as if they are a game, a point-scoring exercise, or uncontrolled warfare.

Use strategic alternatives, tactics, and techniques flexibly. "Mixing and matching" is much better than being rigidly committed to a given approach or a favored bag of tricks.

Don't be squeamish about the deliberate and skillful use of tactics and techniques. There is nothing inappropriate, artificial, or unethical about approaching negotiations well prepared and in a systematic manner. Spontaneity has its place, but it's not a substitute for planning.

Remember! There is nothing in the tenets of responsible professional behavior that requires you to be a victim or an easy mark.

Don't personalize issues—it is usually counterproductive. And don't confuse the outcome of negotiations with personal victory or defeat.

Don't be afraid to fail. A bad agreement may be much worse than no agreement.

Remember! Negotiation is but one mode of conflict management—and it is not always feasible or appropriate.

For negotiations to conclude with all parties being relatively satisfied is usually a much-to-be-desired result.

Although strategies, tactics, and techniques are of great importance, they are not substitutes for responsible goals, decency, and reasonableness.

SUMMARY

In this chapter we discussed the dynamics of negotiation. This included the basic substrategies (distributive and integrative) as well as the requisites, the phases and major tactics and techniques. We also commented on the similarities and differences between representational-symmetrical, representational-asymmetrical, and one-on-one negotiatory transactions.

Finally, attention was directed to human service worker-nonvoluntary client interactions and role conflicts within a conflict management context.

NOTES

1. These definitions are taken from Brown (1977, pp. 276-279).

2. The research by Pruitt and Johnson is cited by Rubin and Brown (1975, pp. 283-284).

3. The first three are discussed in Pruitt and Lewis (1977, pp. 163-166), while the fourth one is commented upon in Kriesberg (1982, p. 218).

4. The advantages of an integrative approach are discussed by Pruitt and Lewis (1977, p. 163).

5. The terms *issue control* and *issue rigidity* are attributed to Fisher by Deutsch (1977, p. 370).

6. For a discussion of this point, see Deutsch (1977, p. 371).

7. This technique, suggested by Fisher, is discussed in Pruitt and Lewis (1977, p. 158).

8. For a discussion of various of the points covered in this section, see Deutsch (1977, pp. 126-138) and Rubin and Brown (1975, p. 155).

9. These points are discussed by Rubin and Brown (1975, pp. 280-288).

10. These propositions are discussed in Tedeschi and Bonoma (1977, pp. 236-237).

11. For a discussion of countermeasures, see Bacharach and Lawler (1981, p. 82).

12. We are indebted to Bacharach and Lawler (1981, pp. 171-174) for these ideas about bluffing.

13. Discussed in Gulliver (1979, pp. 164-165).

14. This tactic, and its rules, as summarized by Linscell, are discussed in Pruitt and Lewis (1977, p. 127).

15. Karrass (1979, pp. 221-224) makes some interesting suggestions regarding what should and should not be done when negotiating by telephone.

16. Extensive lists of specific techniques can be found in Karrass (1979); also see Fisher and Ury (1981), Nierenbeg (1968), and books on collective bargaining.

17. These definitions are taken from Rubin and Brown (1975, pp. 276-277).

18. This concept is taken from Fisher and Ury (1981, p. 161).

19. See Murdach (1980, pp. 458-461) and Cingolani (1984, pp. 442-446).

Chapter 9

INDIRECT OR PROCEDURAL MEANS
AND THE EXERCISE
OF AUTHORITY/POWER

With the completion of the discussion on negotiation, we turn to the last two modes of conflict management to be reviewed in this volume: the use of indirect or procedural means and the exercise of authority or power.

The strategies and tactics employed in these two modes are relatively discrete. However, they do have one important element in common: In neither mode is there reliance on an initial *direct agreement* between the disputants. By agreement we refer to a voluntary process, not coerced compliance. It is true that an agreement may be forthcoming as a result of the use of indirect means, such as calling upon a third party. When direct voluntary agreement between the adversaries is not feasible or desired, indirect or procedural means may be employed.

When the mode of conflict management is authoritative decision making or the exercise of power, there is the implication either that no voluntary direct agreement could be reached, or that such a method of conflict resolution was not deemed appropriate or desirable by one or both of the parties. Thus it may be said that both modes of conflict management described in this chapter are alternatives to a voluntary agreement or a deadlock (potential or actual) between the opponents. Of course, they are also substitutes for unregulated struggle. In other words they are, to a greater or lesser extent, rule-regulated, even if the rules may not always appear desirable or equitable (e.g., "right" of an administrator to resolve unilaterally a conflict by means of the exercise of authority).

CONFLICT MANAGEMENT BY INDIRECT OR PROCEDURAL MEANS

When are indirect or procedural means used to manage conflicts? Such strategies are employed either (a) when the contenders are unable or don't wish to reach an agreement through direct transactions, or (b) when there is dissatisfaction with the result of a previous agreement, thus leading to the decision to use indirect or procedural means instead. The invoking of such strategies implies, of course, either a willingness or a requirement to use them. The requirement to use these means, when it exists, is normally based on convention (norms), administrative rules, or the law. In some instances the mutual decision to use such strategies is itself the product of a direct agreement. For instance, parties to a dispute may decide (agreement) that since they can't resolve their conflict by reaching an accord on the issues, they will rely on a "procedural" solution (e.g., appeals body, voting, etc.). Indirect means also have their own set of relevant strategies, tactics, and techniques.

THE USE OF THIRD PARTIES

There are a variety of third-party roles and functions involved in conflict situations. The function of an audience has already been discussed. Others include advocate; *tertius gaudent* ("enjoying third party"), that is, the potential ally for whose support each party competes to the advantage of this third party (Caplow, 1968, p. 20); consultants; and teachers of conflict management skills. There are also enforcers (e.g., a police officer stopping a family fight); go-betweens (intermediaries) (Kriesberg, 1982, p. 267); and conciliators, whose function is to try to bring the disputants together (e.g., in family courts). In addition, there is the arbitrator, who makes a determination designed to settle or judge a dispute. There are, of course, provisions for third-party involvement, under given circumstances, in various forms of contractual agreements (e.g., labor-management).

Although all of the above roles and functions are worth further consideration, logistic limitations make this impractical. Hence our focus will be on third-party activities and roles particularly relevant to human service organizations, that is, *mediation*, the use of an *ombudsman*, the use of *consultation*, and the *teaching* of conflict management skills.

Mediation

Mediation is a tactic involving the use of conciliatory and facilitative processes by a third party, a mediator. The desired outcome or expectation in respect to the mediation is a settlement that the disputants were unable or unwilling to achieve by themselves, at least in a given period of time (Kriesberg, 1982, p. 266). This last proviso suggests that "speeding up" the resolution of a conflict may be one of the anticipated functions of a mediator. In our usage, mediation is a voluntary process that may be structured or informal. The basic function of the mediator is to facilitate the process likely to lead to a satisfactory resolution, and to assist the parties to the conflict in working through the substance of the dispute.

For mediation to succeed, both parties must want a solution and have confidence in the mediator. Mediation seems to work best when the power differential between the contenders is not too great (Bernard, 1957, p. 111). Experience has also shown that mediators often find it useful to meet with the concerned parties (individuals or teams) in both separate and joint sessions (Pruitt & Lewis, 1977, p. 207).

The major activities by a mediator include the following:

(a) providing a suitable and neutral physical/psychological setting that will optimize the likelihood of a constructive approach to the dispute by the participants

(b) supporting helpful interpersonal attitudes and encouraging a problem-solving orientation

(c) assisting one or both parties to "loosen" their grip on rigidly held positions by (1) developing a "circumventing" formula, that is, a way around obstacles; (2) making it clear what concessions are realistic and encouraging appropriate concessional exchanges or substitutions; (3) aiding in the development of "mutual gain" options (integrative agreements) that will profit both sides

(d) employing pressure (e.g., time limits, fear of an outraged public) to reduce unreasonable demands and modify intransigent attitudes

Some specific techniques are listed in the following Action Guide.

Action Guide for the Mediator!

(1) Establish specific ground rules, norms (including those of fairness and responsibility) and appropriate procedures.
   (a) Offer approval for legitimate activities and disapprove of questionable ones.
   (b) Build trust, confidence and construct adequate communication mechanisms.
(2) Provide information, offer ideas, and test assertions.
(3) Suggest compromises that the disputants might not have thought of, or that they would be unwilling to suggest (e.g., might be seen as a sign of weakness if they originated with one of the contenders).
(4) Assist in the face-maintenance process.

(5) Serve as a "sponge" for the emotional catharsis requirements of the parties, thus reducing personal invectives between them.

(6) Clarify, analyze, and summarize the discussion.

(7) Maximize commonalities.

(8) Reduce misattributed or "false" elements in the conflict.

(9) Provide for "cooling off" periods.

(10) Clarify priorities and restate or redefine issues.

(11) Identify interests behind positions.

(12) Suggest ways in which additional benefits might be put on the table.

(13) Invent or aid the disputants to invent mutual gain options.

(14) Build support for an agreement.

(15) Publicly praise the agreement as well as the contenders for their "responsible behavior."

(16) Facilitate a constructive atmosphere and appropriate physical arrangements.

The overall contributions of mediation include increasing the considered range of possible "solutions," reducing irrationalities, improving process skills and communications, regulating "costs" (including those involving "face"), and serving as a psychological pressure source for agreement:

Effective third party interventions generally create pressures toward agreement. These pressures drive bargainers to make concessions and narrow the differences between them, or at least to demonstrate that they have given serious consideration to alternatives to their initially preferred positions. Authoritativeness and impartiality, as these affect confidence and trust in a third party, seem to be foundations of effective intervention. (Rubin & Brown, 1975, p. 63)[1]

Although there is much emphasis in the writings on mediation in respect to the requirement that the mediator be impartial and neutral as a condition of gaining trust and effectiveness, the matter is not as clear-cut as may appear. Certainly, a biased, manipulative mediator is undesirable and likely to provoke resistance and resentment. However, "pure" neutrality and disinterestedness on the part of the mediator are probably idealized characteristics and somewhat misleading expectations. The following perceptive comment by Gulliver (1979, pp. 213-124) puts the matter into a realistic perspective:

The intervention of a mediator turns the initial dyad of a dispute into a triadic interaction of some kind. The disputing parties retain their ability to decide whether or not to agree to and accept proposals for an outcome, irrespective of the source of proposals. Yet clearly the mediator exercises influence in some degree, whether he remains largely passive or virtually controls the exchange of information and the learning process. He becomes a negotiator and as such, he inevitably brings with him, deliberately or not, certain ideas, knowledge, and assumptions, as well as certain interests and concerns of his own and those of other people whom he represents. Therefore he is not, and cannot be, neutral and merely a catalyst. He not only affects the interaction but, at least in part, seeks and encourages an outcome that is tolerable to him in terms of his own ideas and interests. He may even come into conflict with one or both of the parties.

At the very least, a mediator usually has a stake in the outcome being successful insofar as failure by the parties to reach an agreement may reflect negatively on his or her own competency. Clearly, the mediator cannot be viewed as value-free. Nevertheless, it greatly enhances the effectiveness of mediators if they are perceived as being basically fair and reasonable.

There has been a marked increase, in recent years, of conflict managing structures as alternatives to courts or the unilateral exercise of power. We will consider these new structures under the overall heading of "Dispute Resolution Centers and Services." One of the major tactics employed in the work of these centers and services is mediation. Although there has been a history in various countries of applying mediation, conciliation, and arbitration procedures to industrial disputes, the expansion of the concept to such areas of conflict as minor criminal or civil disputes is innovative (at least in many Western countries). These new programs provide mediation in realms as diverse as landlord-tenants disputes, conflicts between consumers and merchants, domestic crises, neighborhood controversies, hostage dramas, divorce settlements, conflicts between ethnic/racial groups, alleged violations of equal opportunity laws, hospital-patient disputes, and conflicts within school systems (McGillis, 1981, p. 35).[2]

In 1980, the U.S. Congress passed the Dispute Resolution Act for "establishing and evaluating innovative alternative approaches to dispute settlements." Shortly thereafter, two private foundations (Ford and Hewlett), funded the creation of a new, nonprofit National Institute for Dispute Resolution. In addition, some states have passed laws providing for comparable services, and centers have been set up in neighborhoods and within organizations. Significantly, the chief justice of the U.S. Supreme Court issued a "plea for increased use of mediation and arbitration rather than dependence on the courts for the resolution of social and interpersonal disputes and conflicts" (Brown, 1982, p. 2).

A wide variety of educational programs has been initiated for those being prepared to serve as mediators. In some instances, these training arrangements have been aimed at persons who are already qualified in occupations such as social work, psychology, or law, while in other programs volunteers are being prepared to serve a third-party function in neighborhood disputes. The tremendous growth of these services, along with supporting structures and programs, appears to justify the use of the phrase, "the dispute resolution movement."

The use of dispute centers and mediation processes in new areas of activity constitutes an important social innovation in many Western contexts. However, it should be recognized that in various other societies (and subcultures and religious groups) the use of mediation in many spheres is not a new development. I recently watched a real-life example of the conciliation/mediation process at work in the People's Republic of China (via TV). The situation involved a domestic dispute with divorce as a potential outcome. The result, which was strongly welcomed by the mediators and other officials, was a decision by the couple in conflict to remain together. However, the techniques employed were of a psychologically coercive nature in which the social control elements and the societal expectations and "requirements" predominated. The procedures employed were incompatible with what many divorce mediators in countries such as the United States and Australia would define as appropriate or acceptable.

The function of the mediator in dispute resolution structures is usually to try, through voluntary means, to assist the contending parties in the dispute to arrive at as mutually satisfactory an outcome as possible. As one writer put it, in regard to divorce mediation, the "purpose of winning a case or providing treatment is replaced by the purpose of facilitating a fair settlement" (Barsky, 1984, p. 102). And, as we have noted at various points in the book, the traditional "helping techniques" of human service workers are frequently not adequate for this task, nor are the standard adversarial orientations and competencies of lawyers. This will become clear by examination of a process familiar to many human service practitioners— divorce mediation.

Family disputes often reach a pitch of considerable ferocity. A research study found that the more intimate a relationship the more intense conflict will be within that relationship, and the more extreme the disputing styles (Alford, 1982, pp. 361-374). It is no wonder that the police often approach such disputes with great caution. In recent years there has even been a campaign of violence in Australia against family court judges. It is not surprising that the adversarial mode, characteristic of the judicial process, has been called into serious question in regard to its appropriateness in the arena of divorce. The accompanying chart, comparing the adversarial and mediational approaches to divorce, is illuminating. Its author, Daniel G. Brown, is a strong proponent of mediation.

In order to further illuminate the nature of mediation, it is useful to distinguish between divorce therapy and divorce mediation. Divorce therapy is primarily concerned with assisting the parties involved in the disengagement process to cope with a variety of intense emotions (e.g., anger, guilt, anxiety, rejection, depression) often associated with divorce. Assistance is also provided the parties in coming to terms, psychologically, with the new situation, as well as with understanding what happened and why—and in looking at future problems and options.

> Divorce therapy may be differentiated from divorce mediation in that the former is focused more on stress relief, individual behavior change and increased self-understanding, while the latter is focused more on dealing with specific problems, resolving disputes and negotiating differences inherent in the dissolution of the marital state. While successful divorce therapy may facilitate mediation and while successful mediation may be therapeutic, these two processes should be clearly separated. (Brown, 1982, pp. 30-31)

One other point should be made in respect to this distinction: Some people see the therapeutic-counseling approach as manipulative and controlling. For such a person the very suggestion that he or she see a "counselor" may be threatening, since it is seen as putting the person at a disadvantage in comparison with the partner (if the latter is perceived as being comfortable with the therapeutic type of interaction). In such circumstances, the mediational approach may be much more acceptable and effective.

Among the subroles commonly performed by divorce mediators are those of convener, intermediary, reality checker, conflict manager, interpreter, clarifier, information supplier, persuader, harmonizer, and teacher. Within these roles, specific techniques employed include setting tone and creating climate; improving communications; emphasizing areas of agreement as well as identifying difference that still require attention; providing for the controlled ventilation of feelings; reframing questions and restating comments with reduced affect, serving as a verbal "buffer zone"; and providing positive reinforcements.

Overall, the evaluations of divorce mediation and related dispute resolution services have been favorable.[3] In addition to saving time and money, mediation also seems to have other beneficial results. For example, a preliminary evaluation of the Denver Custody Mediation Project reported the following results:

(a) A total of 80% of the mediated couples were able to reach agreement during or following mediation, compared to about 50% of the control group (nonmediated).

(b) Joint legal custody outcome was much more common than was one-parent custody among the mediated, but the situation was reversed in respect to nonmediated couples.

CHART 9.1
Adversarial and Mediational Approaches to Divorce

Factor	Adversarial	Mediational
Definition of the issues	Strongly influenced by attorneys	Defined by divorcing parties
Legal framework	Marital dissolution: John Doe vs. Mary Doe	Marital dissolution: John and Mary Doe
Who is the client?	The husband or the wife	The family (divorcing couple and children)
Relationship of divorcing parties to each other	Focus on past; blame, mistrust, revenge; communication minimal or nonexistent	Focus on current issues, restructuring family relations; communication preserved
Relationship of divorcing parents to their children	Creates conflicts, adjustment problems, divided loyalties	Focus on preserving parent-child relations and postdivorce co-parenting arrangements
Children	Not the concern of attorney; focus not on parent-child relationships	Primary concern of mediator; focus on "parents are forever"
Child Custody/Visitation	Court decides	Parents decide
Anger, hostility	Rekindled, tend to increase and intensify	Defused, tend to decrease and weaken
Stress, emotional trauma	Prolonged, tend to increase	Shortened, tend to lessen
Expense of divorce to parties	Usually more, sometimes much more	Usually less, sometimes much less
Time to reach settlement	More, longer delay	Less, as rapidly as couple desire
Court costs and time	More time and more tax dollars	Reduces time and saves tax dollars
Confidentiality	Not maintained; public exposure in court	Maintained; no public exposure
Expectations re: settlement	Strongly influenced by attorneys	Those of divorcing parties
Goal and desired outcome	Win: give as little as possible and get as much as possible	A fair, equitable, mutually acceptable agreement made by parties themselves
Decision re: final settlement	Made by a judge	Made by the divorcing parties themselves
Adherence to terms of divorce by the parties	Less likely, since the terms are imposed by outside authority (judge)	More likely since the terms are those agreed to by the parties themselves
Postdivorce disputes	More likely	Less likely

SOURCE: This chart is reproduced, with permission, from Daniel G. Brown, "Divorce and Family Mediation: History, Review, Future Directions," Conciliation Courts Review, Vol. 20 (No. 2), December 1982, pp 1-41.

(c) Mediated cases, when compared with nonmediated ones, also showed greater improvement in the relationships between the exspouses, more coparenting and participation with the children, fewer postdivorce problems, and less litigation.

Of course, not all the evidence is in yet. And some concern has been articulated to the effect that divorce mediation is being treated as a trendy panacea. Also, fears have been expressed that some lawyers may find themselves in an ethical bind because of the potential clash of interests in "representing" both parties in a dispute. In addition, mediators may sometimes exploit or coerce clients in the guise of responsible mediation (Brown, 1982).

There are indications that the mediation process doesn't work as effectively with those with less education and those from a lower socioeconomic status, when compared with the more advantaged. Also, persons who suffer from drug/alcohol abuse or serious psychological problems do not appear to be good candidates for the mediational approach (McGillis, 1981, p. 38). A study of divorcing couples at the Family Mediation Center in Atlanta found that four factors inhibited or made the mediation process more difficult. These factors were (a) a high degree of interpersonal or intrapersonal conflict, (b) insufficient material resources to be divided, (c) a lack of familiarity with the requirements of mediation, and (d) a marked power differential pattern between the parties in matters such as decision making and control of finances (Brown, 1982, p. 32).

In short, it may be said that many of the "new" conflict managing structures and processes using the mediational tactic hold much promise, if used appropriately, and if the personnel involved are sufficient in number and possess the necessary competencies. It is important, though, to appreciate the fact that these innovations are not cure-alls, and that some additional unanticipated difficulties are likely to be identified as time passes. Careful monitoring, coupled with disciplined enthusiasm rather than uncritical admiration, is called for. Certainly, human service workers, if provided with the appropriate conflict managing education and training, would seem to be excellent candidates for many of the key roles in these new "social devices."

We have emphasized, in the immediately preceding discussion, mediational activities associated with divorce and like situations. However, much mediation occurs at different "levels"—between workers and management, at the societal/community level (e.g., mediating a racial conflict to try to head off a "race riot"), or between nations.

The actual dynamics of the mediational negotiating process in all of the situations and levels we have mentioned have much in common, despite some significant differences. For instance, political pressures and the impact of public opinion are, obviously, more relevant considerations when the mediator is functioning in a worker-management, community/societal, or international relations sphere of activity, than in a divorce situation. Nevertheless, differences in the circumstances should not obscure the similarities in the methods employed by the mediators in all the various spheres in which they function.

If mediation is to be an appropriate and effective mechanism of conflict management, certain conditions must obtain. For instance, there must be a type of dispute that is perceived to be accessible to mediation. And the selection of this form of conflict management must be seen by the adversaries as being acceptable and no less in their interests than other available options. These points are effectively made in the following extract from an editorial that appeared in the *Age* (Melbourne, Australia) newspaper on April 18, 1986 (p. 13).

> Mediate? Fine, But What About . . .
>
> . . . Mediation between the United States and Libya may seem like a good idea at a time when there is an urgent need to prevent more violence. . . . But could mediation achieve anything at this stage? . . . For mediation to proceed it must first be established that there is a dispute. Libya, despite overwhelming evidence that it sponsors international terrorism, still refuses to accept that there is a case for Colonel Gaddafi to answer. The Libyan Government regards itself as an innocent party attacked by a superpower. How could there be any mediation, the Libyans would say, when there is nothing to discuss except American brutality?

The difficulties in trying to mediate in such a situation are only too apparent.

In summary, then, mediation is a key tactic within the framework of the third-party strategy. It is a tactical skill that is increasingly in demand. But, like other methods of conflict management, it is effective only under appropriate circumstances.

Teaching Conflict Management Competencies

The human service worker may be called upon to instruct clients and other interested parties in the use of conflict management techniques and skills. The instruction may include consciousness raising in regard to "conflict blind" areas; exposure to a range of conflict management tactics, techniques, and styles; and planning for management of the conflict that is the source of concern (Frey, 1979, p. 129). Such instruction is often necessary because reliance on habitual coping mechanisms (even if ineffectual), and tunnel vision in regard to options, are common responses to conflict situations.[4]

Frey (1979, pp. 129-131) identifies eight steps that may be involved in helping clients to be better able to manage the conflicts that confront them. These are (a) building trust, (b) affirming personal strength, (c) sending and receiving accurate messages, (d) testing reality, (e) setting goals, (f) generating alternatives, (g) selecting alternatives, and (h) planning for implementation. In a similar vein, a family mediator speaks of teaching the mediation process to clients and lists requisite techniques and competencies such as "brainstorming," confronting, compromise, role reversal, and the "nuances of timing" (Barsky, 1984, p. 103).

It has also been suggested that attention be directed toward the "prevention of dysfunctional conflicts" by teaching conflict management skills to children in schools and by providing group education for adults, along the lines of the parenting classes that are now offered (Frey, 1979, p. 136).[5]

The Use of Consultants in Conflict Management

Another third party who may be used in a tactical way in conflict management situations is the consultant. The consultant may serve as a coach to one or the other of the parties in the conflict. Or, in the guise of a disinterested outsider or expert, the consultant may be misused as a "weapon" by one of the adversaries. Some expert witnesses (e.g., psychiatrists) are employed in this manner in courtrooms.

A consultant may also be employed objectively to analyze a conflict or potential conflict situation and to recommend preventive or remedial action. It is not unusual for a troubled organization to use a consultant for this purpose. However, a risk confronting the consultant who is so employed is that of being manipulated into serving a partisan function on behalf of the interests of certain of the participants. Any consultant who is involved in conflict management must take particular pains to avoid this trap.

The Use of an Ombudsman in Conflict Management

The ombudsman may be employed as a third party to assist in conflict management. Although the role of the ombudsman is frequently much more inclusive than just this function, it is the third-party conflict management activity of the ombudsman in which we are particularly interested. From its original meaning in Scandinavia, the concept of the ombudsman has become quite diffuse, a fact that disturbs some students of the subject.[6] The "technical" usage is that the ombudsman is a politically neutral officer of the legislature (by whatever name) who reviews and investigates complaints against administrative actions submitted by members of the public. The main instruments of the office are fact finding, persuasion, criticism, and publicity (Rowat, 1968, p. 36).

Although it is true that the indiscriminate use of the term may erode its essential meaning, the popularity of the concept, in its diverse forms and various societal and organizational contexts, suggests that there is a key element in the idea that has met a widespread "felt need." We are sympathetic to the wider meaning of ombudsman, even if it represents a partial "corruption" of the original idea. Thus we shall consider the ombudsman to be a duly empowered complaint-handling individual whose primary activities and skills involve fact finding and persuasion, with resort to publicity in some circumstances. It is vital that the ombudsman not be in the "pocket" of an organization's administrator. Hence a basic independence and autonomy is a necessary requisite of the position.

Depending upon the situation, the ombudsman may be viewed as a part of the formal appeals mechanism or as an "institutionalized," albeit informal, method of ensuring fairness and effectiveness in an organization. We believe that the use of the ombudsman in organizations is an important component in the conflict management systems of such bodies. It is our observation that there are numerous situations in human service organizations involving conflicts between staff and administrators, staff and staff, and clients/students and staff, which would greatly profit from the use of an ombudsman.

Some of the objections we have encountered to the establishment of ombudsman positions include:

(a) It is unnecessary since there are formal appeal structures.
(b) Counselors and/or sympathetic health service/personnel department staff can and do provide an equivalent service.
(c) It impinges unduly on the responsibilities and rights of various administrators.
(d) It will tend to increase the workload of administrators and may "incite" people to use the appeals system.
(e) The idea of having such a position in a benevolent nonprofit organization is virtually an insult to a humane organization and demonstrates a lack of confidence in its leadership.
(f) It is difficult to ensure that the position of the ombudsman is truly an "independent" one.

Of all the above objections, we believe that only the last one has significant merit. The first of the objections overlooks the fact that many persons are intimidated by formal appeal structures or are not aware of how to "get into the system." Also, in some cases, particularly those of a highly personal nature, the formal appeals system may be seen as being too "public."

One of the ombudsman's more important functions is to assist people to use the formal structures, including appeals systems, more effectively. Additionally, the ombudsman can work quietly and does not have the authority to impose sanctions.

The second objection confuses the counseling function with the fact-finding, investigatory one. They are fundamentally different. Also, personnel department employees are usually not independent of the administration. This is not to deny the fact that various individuals may provide an ombudsmanlike function, on a personal basis, on occasions. However, this is quite a different matter from having a regularized position for handling such matters. The third objection goes to the heart of the matter, since administrators themselves may be anything but independent or neutral third parties. Hence administrators who act as ombudsmen may find that they are in the position of having to investigate themselves. The answer to the fourth objection is that using an appeals system is not like buying a new car. It is not a pleasure in itself, and the feared "overuse" is most likely to represent a real need for assistance.

The fifth objection assumes that in a nonprofit "benevolent organization" conflicting interests and genuine disputes do not exist. This is patently not the case. Benevolence is best assured when it is backed by appropriate rights protecting, conflict managing mechanisms.

The final objection does raise an important issue, since in the original conception of the ombudsman the individual filling that position would represent, and be supported by, a different body (i.e., legislature) than that about which complaints were raised (i.e., the governmental bureaucracy). Nevertheless, there are various ways around this problem, even if none of them is perfect. One device is to set up a body (e.g., a high-level committee external to the organization) to serve in a supervisory manner. Another solution—one that doesn't provide as much autonomy, however—is to have the ombudsman directly responsible to a board of management, or to a superordinate organizational body, rather than to the administration of the organization. Even imperfect "solutions" often prove clearly preferable to having no ombudsman. Certainly the support of top management is essential for the ombudsman mechanism to work.

In a survey conducted by the Harvard Business Review, less than 1 respondent in 10 reported that his or her company had an ombudsman, but nearly two-thirds of this minority (that had such a position) rated the person high or medium-high in effectiveness (Ewing, 1978, pp. 169-170). Our judgment coincides with this finding. It appears that in many situations the ombudsman position is an invaluable adjunct to other conflict management structures.

THE USE OF QUASI-JUDICIAL AND JUDICIAL APPEAL MECHANISMS AS A STRATEGY IN CONFLICT MANAGEMENT

In some situations persons involved in conflicts have recourse to the formal legal system as a means of bringing about the resolution of a controversy. A key function of the law is, of course, resolving disputes (Berman, 1958, p. 31). This is not to suggest that one should turn to the courts too readily: Expense, delays, complexities, and the adversarial mode often make such action difficult, frustrating, and sometimes unsatisfactory. Yet the right to appeal to a court is an indispensable safeguard. However, because the formal judicial system is a full subject in itself, we shall concentrate in this section on quasi-judicial mechanisms. In so doing we are not in any way minimizing the use of the courts as a critical part of the conflict management system.

It is worth noting that an organization "is more likely than an individual to make a complaint about an individual, and it is also more likely to complain about an individual than another organization" (Black, 1976, p. 101). In general, in a conflict situation between an employee and an organization, the odds clearly favor the organization. Most organizations are still quite autocratic in conception and structure—and many basic rights, including due process (or "natural justice"), often do not apply to the employee (Ewing, 1978). The situation appears to be gradually improving, though, and knowledge of what access to the courts is, or is not, available should be an important part of the conflict managing process. This applies to those working in human service organizations as well as in others. Although unionized employees tend to be less vulnerable than those who aren't unionized, even they frequently lack adequate protection in regard to their rights within an organization.

The practical difficulties and uncertain legal basis for using the formal judicial system in certain types of disputes have led to the development of quasi-judicial appeal processes in organizations as mechanisms for conflict management (and the protection of rights). Appeals systems within organizations are essentially of three basic types: those set up by legislation (e.g., appeal boards for clients of certain public human service organizations); those grievance processes negotiated by unions (or other employee groups) with management; and those that have been set up by organizations themselves at their own initiative. The third mechanism is, basically, a system set up and maintained by an organization in order to provide organizational members with "an avenue of appeal when they think they have been treated unjustly by an agent of the organization"(Scott, 1965, p. vi). Appeal systems of this type have emerged from a questioning of traditional authority and its prerogatives; a generalized egalitarian/humanistic ideology; the increased power of workers; and a more enlightened mode of management, which includes the employee's need for satisfaction on the job and requires organizational legitimacy.

Some organizational appeal systems are viewed with considerable skepticism by employees (and by clients in respect to appeal mechanisms for users-of-service). Such skepticism is probably well-deserved in certain cases. On the other hand, a good internal appeals system can be a very useful and desirable method for dealing with unresolved conflicts and for the protection of individual rights. Some of the requirements for a fair and effective intraorganizational appeals structure include the following:

(a) It should be institutionalized with a regularized procedure.
(b) It should be perceived as being both equitable and effective.
(c) It should be easy to understand and use.
(d) It should be visible.
(e) It should apply to all employees.[7]

One final comment on this point is necessary. An internal appeals procedures may or may not be subject to further review and enforcement by a court or other outside authority. Nor is it necessary for such an appeals system to always be so accountable. Depending upon the circumstances, and given organizational structure, a self-contained internal appeals mechanism may be adequate, provided that the ultimate legal rights afforded to all persons in the society are not compromised by the existence of the appeals system.

THE USE OF FORMALIZED
DECISION-MAKING PROCEDURES
AS A STRATEGY IN CONFLICT MANAGEMENT: VOTING

The tactic on which we will center our attention is voting. After all, voting is the most common "formalized" *procedural* means within groups for settling differences over *substantive* issues. Who of us has not participated in this activity an almost infinite number of times? Yet its implications, and the surrounding issues, are not quite as clearly perceived as might be expected.

Voting is not only a *procedure* for managing conflict and reaching a decision, it is also an *expression* of conflict and, in some cases, even a *conflict generator*. In the earlier discussion on consensual decision making, we pointed out that in given situations, and in certain cultures, voting is seen as unduly provocative and even embarrassing. After all, it is a competitive device and results in winners and losers. Those who are victorious are likely to experience pleasure, while those on the losing side often have a sense of displeasure, loss of self-esteem, or even anger. In contrast to persuasion and comparable tactics, voting does not primarily aim at changing people's beliefs, feelings, or even positions. It is based on numbers, rather than the inherent validity of arguments, or the rationality of people. For this reason, people often try to avoid voting showdowns. Yet is an invaluable procedure for arriving at a decision when other modes of reaching an agreement don't work or would have unsatisfactory results. Voting can be used to prevent a paralysis in decision making, or even the use of less desirable methods, such as dictatorial decrees or physical aggression.

What may be the unattractive features of voting may, in certain circumstances, be its strength. For instance, voting makes it clear that there are conflicting views or positions; thus it lessens the risk of genuine conflict being masked by "a premature consensus," or "benevolent misperception." A premature consensus—that is, an agreement that results from group pressures (or internalized discomfort)—is not uncommon and often prevents some of the important issues and differences from emerging. And benevolent misperception—that is, intentionally overemphasizing commonalities and minimizing differences in order to reduce conflict and make "progress"—often has the same impact (Deutsch, 1977, p. 364). Voting may be a valuable counter to these "distortions."

Voting has the potential for being misused as a device to force dissenters to come out into the open and be subject to various forms of social control. A secret ballot can reduce this risk. There is, additionally, the danger of manipulation by means of a "straw vote." The straw vote, an informal testing of opinion, may be useful in determining whether differences do exist, and if unifying options are feasible. However, it is sometimes employed to "smoke out" those with deviant views, or to preempt a later opportunity for more formal decision making. In one instance of which I know, a straw vote was later claimed to be an "authentic expression of opinion," resulting in a definitive administrative decision being made on that basis. This was done despite the fact that it was contrary to the understanding of many of those participating in the straw vote.

Some of the potential disadvantages of voting can be compensated for by selective use of "minority reports." The report by an out-voted minority that doesn't wish to join in a decision (including recommendations) favored by the majority is insufficiently used in committees, commissions, and like bodies. The views held by a minority may well prove to be more valid in the long run than those of the dominant group. As the saying goes, "truth is not decided by a vote."

Despite the great usefulness of voting as a decision-making and conflict-resolving mechanism, it is important that there be institutionalized procedures to ensure that minority ideas are not lost by being submerged. Too often minority reports are viewed as disruptive, or as an indication of unsatisfactory work by a committee or its chairperson. It is our view that, if used selectively, the minority report can enhance the quality of decision making. Ground rules of policy-recommending bodies should legitimize the role of such reports, and provision ought to be made to allow minority reports to be transmitted, together with the majority recommendations, to the final decision-making body.

In summary, then, voting provides a very important and useful *procedural* devise for dealing with conflicts that cannot be resolved through substantive agreement. However, voting can be used inappropriately, at the wrong time, or in a manipulative fashion. As is true of other tactics, mechanical application is no substitute for thoughtful and responsible use.

Action Guide!

(1) Don't use voting as a substitute for the full exploration of issues.
(2) Don't use voting in such a formalistic manner that it blocks the reasonable interchange of ideas or lessens the opportunity for agreement by persuasion.
(3) Don't use voting as a club with which to beat down minority views.
(4) Don't gloat when the vote comes out in your favor.
(5) Don't be afraid to use voting as an appropriate procedural mechanism for managing conflict. It can be much more effective and "democratic" than insisting on a consensual decision.

Although our discussion has been limited to voting, it is worth observing that a knowledge of the rules governing the conduct of meetings is a vital aspect of the activities of the human service worker. Skill in performing the various roles required for successful meetings is very important, both for the prevention of unnecessary conflicts and for effectively coping with those that do emerge. And, as one writer has pointed out, many of the same skills, tactics, and techniques used in negotiations, and other conflict managing strategies, are similar to those used in meetings generally (Fletcher, 1983, p. 79).

CONFLICT MANAGEMENT BY THE
EXERCISE OF AUTHORITY/POWER

We shall now briefly discuss the managing of conflict by authoritative or nakedly authoritarian decision making. This mode occurs when one of the parties to a conflict, out of preference or necessity, resolves it by exercising the authority or power residing (or claimed to reside) in the position held by that person in the organization.

In this situation, the problem is not how to reach a settlement of the dispute, since the resolution has been imposed. Rather, the issues associated with this type of conflict management pertain to the consequences for the participants and the organization of such use of authority or power. For instance, what can or should those subject to the authority or power do if they object to the way in which the conflict is settled, or to the substance of the settlement. The selection of tactics employed in enacting this strategy of conflict management is of great importance—as is the choice of tactics that might be used in opposition to the decisions.

By definition, authority is legitimated power. This does not mean that the legitimacy is irrevocable. If those subject to the authority no longer recognize it as legitimate, then the person who possessed the authority may resort to raw power, resign the claimed authority, or strike some sort of quasi-voluntary agreement with those who objected. The "right" of the person in authority to resolve a conflict by authoritative decision making may be accepted, but the means employed may be viewed as unwise, insensitive, unfair, inappropriate, or even illegitimate. Thus the umbrella of legitimacy does not provide the person in authority with *carte blanche* in the enacting of the role. And there is the added possible complication of the person with authority going beyond the realm of the granted authority— extending it beyond the legitimated boundaries. For these reasons, authoritative resolutions of conflict are by no means necessarily tidy, easy, or uncomplicated. And authoritarian solutions relying on power as such are particularly fraught with dangers, including the danger of an ultimate backlash.

The skill with which authoritative decision making is carried out is critical. Just think of the ways in which a conflict-ending decision may be announced—and the different consequences that may eventuate. The authoritative person may say, "I have given the matter considerable thought and believe it should be handled in this way. My reasons are as follows. . . ." Or the decision maker might aggressively proclaim, "This is the way it will be done—and if you don't like it, you know what you can do."

It is, of course, perfectly appropriate—and often necessary—for persons in organizations to make various kinds of definitive decisions, including those resolving conflicts. Such decision making may be a requisite aspect of the person's role, as well as being essential for the effective operation of an organization. Nevertheless, certain of the tactics and techniques used in authoritative decision making in respect to conflict are open to question, in terms of both effectiveness and fairness. Among the less desirable of these are delaying mechanisms, including halting action by inaction (a form of "pocket veto"); withholding requisite information (e.g., restricted circulation of minutes); or simply using strongly coercive power, *force majeure.* The first of these, stalling (by whatever name or technique), may in some situations be more potent (and dangerous or undesirable) than overt opposition. It also avoids the discomfort of a direct confrontation (Kanter, 1985, pp. 232, 243). The other two approaches run the risk of eventually proving to be counterproductive because of the reactions they are likely to provoke at some point in time.

Tactics and techniques, such as those mentioned above and others covered in our earlier discussion of managing conflict by covert means, may be justified under unusual circumstances, but they should normally be avoided. Of course, it is not only the decision makers who may use these tactics. Those subject to authoritative decisions may also employ these types of tactics. And raw "nonlegitimated power" (by a "coalition of the officially powerless") may be forceful enough to override or deflate authoritative conflict management.

We believe that the authoritative resolution of conflict is usually best accomplished by providing a reasoned rationale, by persuading, by bargaining, and by keeping the door open to be influenced by new evidence or arguments. Since it takes two to "tango," reason and persuasion will work only if those affected by such decision making are willing to be so influenced and directed. The process is greatly enhanced if an institutionalized "appeal" process is available for those who wish to challenge a conflict-ending decision.

There are occasions when human service workers in interaction with clients have to rely on the strategy of authoritative decision making to resolve a conflict situation. This is particularly characteristic of transactions with certain types of nonvoluntary clients. In such cases, the setting and enforcement of limits, backed by potentially coercive action, may have to be employed. Even in such instances, keeping "cool," projecting a genuine desire to be understanding and fair, and separating the action from dislike or rejection of the client are important concomitants of the effective and humane use of authority in resolving a conflict.

The following Action Guide suggests ways to reinforce the above comments.

Action Guide!

(1) Don't use the possession of authority as justification for being authoritarian in managing conflict.

(2) Remember, effective authoritative conflict management usually benefits from the same human considerations that are involved in negotiations.

(3) Don't fall into the trap of assuming that by being fair, reasonable, and willing to persuade and be persuaded, your authority in conflictual situations will be impaired.

NOTES

1. An unusual third-party role is that of a "designer," a person who designs an outcome. For a discussion of this designed-outcome approach to conflict resolution, see De Bono (1986).

2. One important structure is the National Center for Dispute Settlement of the American Arbitration Association.

3. See Brown (1982, pp. 18-19, 31-33).

4. Also see Seidl (1977, pp. 269-275).

5. Also see Eleson (1981, pp. 488-493).

6. For authoritative and interesting discussions on the origins, spread, and uses of the "ombudsman" idea, see Anderson (1968).

7. Although Ewing (1978, p. 156) lists these as requirements for "due process," they apply equally to the mechanisms for ensuring that "right."

EPILOGUE

Our discussion of conflict management has now come to an end. It has not been like a morality play in which virtue is always seen as triumphant. The subject is too complex and full of uncertainties for such a moral to be drawn.

To begin with, when diverse interests are in conflict it is not always easy to determine which interests should have priority, or what balance is most equitable. Also, strategies and tactics are not in themselves the answer to structural injustice, or power distortions. Furthermore, our knowledge of conflict management is still very imperfect. The world continues to be full of destructive conflicts at all levels of human interaction. It would be misleading and pretentious not to acknowledge that much more understanding is required about the nature of conflicts and their management. The "track record" to date is simply not good enough.

Strategies, tactics, and techniques are means that can be used on behalf of a variety of ends—good, bad, or indifferent. Hence mastery of technical skills is no substitute for a commitment to prosocial objectives, such as more humane, just, and responsive social arrangements.

It is also important to recognize that winning is not always the ultimate value—or even the best outcome.[1] There are other vital outcomes in life that may be more important. And ethical considerations should always be taken into account in all aspects of conflict management decisions, from whether to engage in conflict to the choice of strategies and tactics. The failure to pay sufficient attention to such matters may also be "instrumentally" harmful by discrediting the ethically insensitive participant.

Finally, we want to stress the fact that conflict management decision should take into account the fact of multiple and diverse outcomes. This diversity results from the fact that different persons, groups, and interests are differentially affected by the results of conflicts and the ways in which they are managed. Additionally, short-, medium-, and long-term outcomes may not always be compatible with each other or with the basic objectives of the conflict management activities. Hence too narrow or short-sighted a perspective in managing conflict may well be self-defeating.

NOTE

1. Some writers on the subject make winning the only objective. We disagree with this approach. For a statement that winning is what it is all about see Colin Rose (1987, p. 12).

REFERENCES

Alford, R. D. (1982). Intimacy and disputing styles within kin and nonkin relationships. *Journal of Family Issues, 3*(3).

Anderson, S. V. (Ed.). (1968). Ombudsmen for American government. *The American Assembly,* Englewood Cliffs, NJ: Prentice-Hall.

Argyle, M. (1983). *The psychology of interpersonal behavior* (4th ed.). Middlesex, England: Penguin Books.

Bacharach, S. B., & Lawler, E. J. (1981). *Bargaining: Power, tactics, and outcomes.* San Francisco: Jossey-Bass.

Barsky, M. (1984). Strategies and techniques of divorce mediation. *Social Casework 65*(2).

Bennis, W. G., Benne, K. D., & Chen, R. (Eds.). (1973). *Interpersonal dynamics* (3rd ed.). Homewood, IL: Dorsey Press.

Berman, H. J. (1958). *The nature and function of law.* New York: Foundation Press.

Bernard, J., et al. (1957). The sociological study of conflict. *The Nature of Conflict.* Paris: UNESCO.

Black, D. (1976). *The behavior of law.* New York: Academic Press.

Brager, G., & Holloway, S. (1978). *Changing human service organizations: Politics and practice.* New York: Free Press.

Brehmer, B., & Hammond, K. (1977). Cognitive factors in interpersonal conflict. In D. Druckman (Ed.), *Negotiations.* Beverly Hills, CA: Sage Publications.

Brown, B. R. (1977). Face-saving and face-restoration in negotiation. In D. Druckman (Ed.), *Negotiations.* Beverly Hills, CA: Sage Publications.

Brown, D. G. (1982). Divorce and family mediation: History, review, future directions. *Conciliation Courts Review 20*(2).

Brown, H., & Murphy, J. (1976). *Persuasion and coercion* (Block 14). Milton Keynes, England: Open University Press.

Caplow, T. (1968). *Two against one: Coalitions in triads.* Englewood Cliffs, NJ: Prentice Hall.

Cingolani, J. (1984). Social conflict perspective on work with involuntary clients. *Social Work* (29).

Collins, B., & Guetzkow, H. (1964). *A social psychology of group processes for decision-making.* New York: John Wiley.

Copeland, M. (1978). *The real spy world.* London: Sphere Books.

Coser, L. A. (1956). *The functions of social conflict.* Glencoe, IL: Free Press.

Dahrendorf, R. (1959). *Class and class in industrial society.* Stanford, CA: Stanford University Press.

Danziger, K. (1976). *Interpersonal communication.* Oxford: Pergamon Press.

Davis, M. S. (1975). *Intimate relations.* New York: Free Press.

De Bono, E. (1986). *Conflicts: A better way to resolve them.* Middlesex, England: Penguin Books.

Deutsch, M. (1977). *The resolution of conflict: Constructive and destructive processes.* New Haven, CT: Yale University Press.

Druckman, D. (1977). Introduction and overview. In D. Druckman (Ed.), *Negotiations.* Beverly Hills, CA: Sage Publications.

Eleson, J. L. (1981). Teaching children to resolve conflict: A group approach. *Social Work* 6(6).

Encyclopedia of Sociology. (1974). Guilford, CT: Dushkin Publishing Group.

Ewing, D. W. (1978). *Freedom inside the organization: Bringing civil liberties to the workplace.* New York: McGraw-Hill.

Feld, S., & Radin, N. (1982). *Social psychology for social work and the mental health professions.* New York: Columbia University Press.

Fisher, R., & Ury, W. (1981). *Getting to yes: Negotiating agreement without giving in.* Boston: Houghton Mifflin.

Fletcher, W. (1983). *Meetings, meetings.* London: Michael Joseph.

Freedman, J. L., Carlsmith, J. M., & Sears, D. O. (1970). *Social psychology.* Englewood Cliffs, NJ: Prentice-Hall.

Frey, D. E. (1979). Understanding and managing conflict. In S. Eisenberg & L. E. Patterson (Eds.), *Helping clients with special concerns.* Chicago: Rand McNally.

Gamson, W. A. (1968). *Power and discontent.* Homewood, IL: Dorsey Press.

Geis, F., & Christie, R. (1970). Machiavellianism and the manipulation of one's fellowman. In K. J. Gergen & D. Marlowe (Eds.), *Personality and social behavior.* Reading, MA: Addison-Wesley.

Gould, J., & Kolb, W. L. (Eds.). (1964). *A dictionary of the social sciences.* Compiled under the auspices of UNESCO. New York: Free Press.

Gulliver, P. H. (1979). *Disputes and negotiations: A cross-cultural perspective.* New York: Academic Press.

Hare, A. P. (1976). *Handbook of small group research* (2nd ed.). New York: Free Press.

Herman, M. G., & Kogan, N. (1977). Effects of negotiators personalities on negotiating behavior. In D. Druckman (Ed.), *Negotiations.* Beverly Hills, CA: Sage Publications.

Himes, J. S. (1980). *Conflict and conflict management.* Athens, GA: University of Georgia Press.

Hopmann, P. T., & Walcott, C. (1977). The impact of external stresses and tensions on negotiations. In D. Druckman (Ed.), *Negotiations.* Beverly Hills, CA: Sage Publications.

Itamachek, D. E. (1982). *Encounters with others.* New York: Holt, Reinhart & Winston.

Kanter, R. M. (1985). *The change masters.* London: Unwin Paperbacks (Counterpoint).

Karrass, C. L. (1979). *The negotiating game.* New York: Thomas Y. Crowell.

Kriesberg, L. (1982). *Social conflicts* (2nd ed.). Englewood Cliffs, NJ: Prentice Hall.

Leavitt, H. J. (1972). *Managerial psychology* (3rd ed.). Chicago: University of Chicago Press.

McClintock, C. G. (1977). Social motivations in settings of outcome interdependence. In D. Druckman (Ed.), *Negotiations.* Beverly Hills, CA: Sage Publications.

McGillis, D. (1981). Delivering everyday justice. *Public Welfare, 39*(4).

Merrill, D. W., & Reid, R. H. (1981). *Personal styles and effective performance.* Radner, PA: Chilton Book Company.

Middleman, R. R., & Goldberg, G. (1974). *Social service delivery: A structural approach to social work practice.* New York: Columbia University Press.

Miller, G. R., & Simons, H. W. (1974). *Perspective on communication in social conflict.* Englewood Cliffs, NJ: Prentice-Hall.

Murdach, A. D. (1980). Bargaining and persuasion with nonvoluntary clients. *Social Work* (25).

Nierenbeg, G. T. (1968). *The art of negotiating*. New York: Hawthorn Books.

Olsen, M. E. (1968). *The process of social organization*. New York: Holt, Rinehart & Winston.

Parsons, T. (Ed.). (1947). *Max Weber: The theory of social and economic organization*. New York: Oxford University Press.

Pruitt, D. G., & Lewis, S. A. (1977). The psychology of integrative bargaining. In D. Druckman (Ed.), *Negotiations*. Beverly Hills, CA: Sage Publications.

Rapoport, A. (1960). *Fights, games, debates*. Ann Arbor: University of Michigan Press.

Raven, B. H., Centers, R., & Rodrigues, A. (1975). The bases of conjugal power. In R. E. Cramwell & D. H. Olsen (Eds.), *Power in families*. New York: Halsted Press.

Raven, B. H., & Kruglanski, A. W. (1970). Conflict and power. In P. Swingle (Ed.), *The structure of conflict*. New York: Academic Press.

Rokeach, M., et al. (1979). *Understanding human values: Individual and societal*. New York: Free Press.

Rose, C. (1987). *Negotiate and win*. Melbourne: Luthian Publishing Company.

Rosenberg, M. (1957). *Occupations and values*. Glencoe, IL: Free Press.

Rowat, D. (1968). The spread of the Ombudsman Idea. In S. V. Anderson (Ed.), *Ombudsmen for American government*. Englewood Cliffs, NJ: Prentice-Hall.

Rubin, J. Z., & Brown, B. R. (1975). *The social psychology of bargaining and negotiation*. New York: Academic Press.

Saks, M. J., & Hastie, R. (1978). *Social psychology in court*. New York: Van Nostrand Reinhold.

Schein, E. H. (1973). Interpersonal communication, group solidarity and social influence. In W. G. Bennis, K. D. Benne, & R. Chen (Eds.), *Interpersonal dynamics* (3rd ed.). Homewood, IL: Dorsey Press.

Scott, W. G. (1965). *The management of conflict: Appeals system in organizations*. Homewood, IL: Richard D. Irwin, Inc., and Dorsey Press.

Seidl, F. W. (1977). Conflict and conflict resolution in residential treatment. *Child Care Quarterly 6*(4).

Sharp, G. (1971). Mechanisms of change in nonviolent action. In H. A. Hornstein et al., *Social intervention*. New York: Free Press.

Shuts, W. C. (1973). Interpersonal underworld. In W. G. Bennis, K. D. Benne, & R. Chen (Eds.), *Interpersonal dynamics* (3rd ed.). Homewood, IL: Dorsey Press.

Steele, F. I. (1973). Physical settings and social interaction. In W. G. Bennis, K. D. Benne, & R. Chen (Eds.), *Interpersonal dynamics* (3rd ed.). Homewood, IL: Dorsey Press.

Strauss, A. L. (1973). Transformations of identities. In W. G. Bennis, K. D. Benne, & R. Chen (Eds.), *Interpersonal dynamics* (3rd ed.). Homewood, IL: Dorsey Press.

Tedeschi, J. T. (Ed.). (1972). *The social influence processes*. Chicago: Aldine-Atherton.

Tedeschi, J. T., & Bonoma, T. V. (1977). Measures of last resort: Coercion and aggression in bargaining. In D. Druckman (Ed.), *Negotiations*. Beverly Hills, CA: Sage Publications.

Terhune, K. W. (1970). The effects of personality in cooperation and conflict. In P. Swingle (Ed.), *The structure of conflict*. New York: Academic Press.

Tilly, C. (1978). *From mobilization to revolution*. Reading, MA: Addison-Wesley.

Whyte, A. (1978). The environment and social behaviour. In H. Tajfel & C. Fraser (Eds.), *Introducing social psychology*. Middlesex, England: Penguin Books.

Zartman, I. W., & Herman, M. R. (1982). *The practical negotiator*. New Haven, CT: Yale University Press.

Zollschan, G. K., & Hirsch, W. (Eds.). (1964). *Explorations in social change*. Boston: Houghton Mifflin.

ABOUT THE AUTHOR

HERB BISNO is Emeritus Professor of Social Work at La Trobe University, Melbourne, Australia. As an authority on Conflict Management in the Human Services, Professor Bisno is asked by universities and government and private agencies to be a guest lecturer and consultant. Previously he was Foundation Professor and Chairman for the Department of Social Work, as well as Deputy Dean of the Behavioral Sciences, at La Trobe University. Before moving to Australia, Professor Bisno was Dean and Professor at the Raymond A. Kent School of Social Work at the University of Louisville. Formerly he was Chairman of Community Service Programs, School of Community Service and Public Affairs at the University of Oregon, as well as Professor of Sociology and Social Welfare. He was a member of the Board of Directors for the Council on Social Work Education and a member of the Commission on Practice for the National Association of Social Workers. He was also a Consultant at the Paul Baerwald School of Social Work at the Hebrew University in Jerusalem, an Advisor to the World Health Organization in Geneva, and United Nations Social Welfare Training Expert to the governments of Indonesia and Turkey. His books include *The Place of the Undergraduate Curriculum in Social Work Education* and *The Philosophy of Social Work*. He has also written numerous book chapters, and many articles for professional journals.